BREAKING
BARRIERS

BREAKING BARRIERS

An African American Family & the Methodist Story

Angella P. Current

Abingdon Press
Nashville

BREAKING BARRIERS:
AN AFRICAN AMERICAN FAMILY AND THE METHODIST STORY

Copyright © 2001 by Abingdon Press

This book is printed on acid-free paper.

Library of Congress Cataloging-in-Publication Data

Current, Angella, 1942-
    Breaking barriers : an African American family & the Methodist story / Angella Current.
        p. cm.
    Includes bibliographical references.
    ISBN 0-687-07036-8
    1. Kelly, Leontine T. C. (Leontine Turpeau Current)   2. United Methodist Church (U.S.)—Bishops—Biography.   3. African American women clergy—Biography.   I. Title.

BX8495.K45 C87 2001
287'.6'092—dc21
[B]

00-067541

01 02 03 04 05 06 07 08 09 10—10 9 8 7 6 5 4 3

MANUFACTURED IN THE UNITED STATES OF AMERICA

Acknowledgments

I am deeply appreciative of the support and encouragement received from the directors, general secretary, and colleagues at the General Board of Higher Education and Ministry. I will always treasure my visits with Dr. Grant and Doris Shockley and Bishop James and Ruth Thomas who affirmed my desire to tell the stories of my family and my family's involvement with the church. I am grateful for the resource support provided by Mt. Zion United Methodist Church historian Carter Bowman, my aunt Anne Brock Turpeau, and the library staff of Garrett Evangelical Theological Seminary; the editorial assistance and listening ears of cousin Ila Beck Hayes Edwards, sister-in-law Yvonne Current, aunt Delores Current Register; and the continuous words of encouragement from members of the Turpeau and Current family and friends. Finally, I will always be grateful for the guidance of the ancestors and the presence of the Holy Spirit throughout this project.

Contents

Foreword

When later authors research and write Methodist and United Methodist Church history, they will find at least one rich resource on a subject that, to date, has not yet been fully developed. That subject is the study of the black families whose contributions to the American social order are so many and so great that they can only be understood as combinations of character, talent, and the grace of God.

Angella Current has made an important contribution to this little-researched area with her account of a remarkably productive black family life. The story would be impressive if it were only a biography of Leontine Turpeau Current Kelly, the first black woman bishop of The United Methodist Church. But this book interweaves Bishop Kelly's story into the larger story of the Turpeau, Bryant, and Current families, as alone and together they made their remarkable contributions to the Church.

It is this interweaving, all within the framework of American segregation and discrimination, that makes this book so important to all Americans, and black Americans in particular. Ms. Current, herself a history major, understands the value of providing for the reader a wider perspective in which to interpret events.

Written in such a manner that any reader will enjoy and be informed by it, this book will be of especial value to several target audiences: young black people whose need for genuine heroes is great, older Church members who will see between these pages the wide range of possibilities that exist for ministry, white church members, whose understanding of black achievement is often limited to sports, entertainment, or some other stereotype, and all pastors who will see the outreach of ministry in four generations of service in the pastorate, in music, in education, in politics, in civil rights, and in the nurturing of family members during both difficult and beneficent times.

As one reviews the current books and articles available on black people—most of which treat the group in impersonal, sociological, statistical terms—it is important to note and to appreciate individual biographies and autobiographies. It is even more important to understand that all outstanding persons come from families and that the full stories of those families need to be told. The interrelations with other families and the joint contributions of family connections are indispensable contributions to individual, familial, and collective achievement.

Leontine Turpeau Current Kelly's place in history is secure. Now, with this book from Angella Current, the reader is privileged to further perceive the profound significance of the family's role in Bishop Kelly's development. In this sense, this text is both a challenge and an inspiration.

Bishop James S. Thomas

Introduction

On December 1, 1985, I joined the staff of the United Methodist General Board of Higher Education and Ministry as the Assistant General Secretary for the Office of Loans and Scholarships at the invitation of Dr. Thomas Trotter, General Secretary. I was the first African American to hold this position, and in 1988, when Dr. Roger W. Ireson became General Secretary, I was promoted to Associate General Secretary.

During my early years at the Board, I encountered many lay and clergy persons within the denomination who expressed that they had not met many Methodists of African American descent, or who were under the impression that many African Americans became Methodist when The United Methodist Church was formed in 1968.

As a fourth-generation Methodist whose paternal great-grandfather was ordained in the West Texas Conference of the Methodist Episcopal Church in 1892 and whose maternal grandfather was ordained in the Delaware Conference of the Methodist Episcopal Church in 1902, I was surprised that in spite of the writings of noted African American Methodist church historians and theologians, such as Lewis V. Baldwin, J. H. Graham, William B. McClain, Grant S. Shockley, and Bishop James S. Thomas, many people were still unaware of the contributions made by African Americans to the Methodist Church and the important role the denomination has played in the empowerment of people, specifically African Americans in the United States and throughout the world.

On the other hand, there were many within the denomination who had met my mother, Leontine Turpeau Current Kelly, or had heard of her amazing journey into the ministry following the death of her minister-husband, James David Kelly, in 1968, or her historic election in 1984 as the first African American woman bishop of The United Methodist Church. A review of Methodist history during the nineteenth and twentieth centuries will show that, without question, the Civil Rights Movement and the Woman's Movement had major influences on the Church; these influences are reflected in the increased representation of racial ethnics and women in leadership roles on all levels, lay and clergy, of the denomination at the close of the twentieth century. By the late 1960s and early 1970s, lay and clergy men and women within The United Methodist Church were calling for an inclusive Church; a Church that recognized the spiritual, organizational, and administrative gifts and graces of racial ethnics and women called to the ordained ministry; and a Church willing to appoint these persons not only to serve local churches, but also to serve in cross-racial appointments as district superintendents and, yes, even in the episcopacy.

Leontine Turpeau Current Kelly's own journey into the ministry, described in this book, is just one example of how God continuously moves through history. Although she became the women's candidate for the episcopacy in 1980 and 1984 and though women and racial ethnic caucuses were approached to support her candidacy, many of us believe, and know, that her ascendancy to such a high office was providential—for it could not have happened if God had not so ordained it!

Leontine was raised in and influenced by the black church and the black community. She was born into a family rooted in Methodism, grounded in an understanding of and a strong faith in God's love, and was committed to ensuring that all persons are given dignity and value and are entitled to maximize their God given potential. Though her call to the ordained ministry and her subsequent election to the episcopacy are unique, there are aspects of her life story that mirror the experience of many women of her generation. Her experiences also reflect those of numerous African Americans whose lives were influenced by the black church, historically black colleges, and the belief that America can fulfill its promise to ensure freedom, justice, and equality for all Americans.

This book was written for many reasons. First, it was important to me that members of The United Methodist Church—including seminarians, pastors, historians, educators, sociologists, and the general public—have a better understanding, and hopefully, an appreciation of the important role African American Methodists have played in the denomination's mission and ministry.

Second, it was important to tell Leontine Turpeau Current Kelly's life story within the context of her family's active involvement in the Methodist Church and the complexities and contradictions family members faced as they ministered and contributed to the African American community in an age of a legally segregated society while simultaneously choosing to believe in and remain connected to a denomination that remained segregated until 1968.

Third, the book describes the societal dynamics and the role the Methodist Church played in the lives of African Americans from the period of Reconstruction through the Civil Rights Era. At the same time, the book explores the human relationships, interconnections, and providential weavings of key persons to one another through their ministries, marriages, and leadership roles within the church and society and their influence upon Leontine's own journey.

CHAPTER ONE

The Baptism

It was June 3, 1920, and the annual meeting of the Washington Conference of the Methodist Episcopal Church had been in session for three days. The delegates of this second Negro Mission Conference, which was established in 1868 by the General Conference of the Methodist Episcopal Church,[1] represented black churches located as far north as Pennsylvania, as far south as Virginia, in the District of Columbia, Maryland, and West Virginia. Dressed in their best clothes, ministers, their wives and children, and lay delegates gathered once again at their favorite meeting site on the campus of Morgan College in Baltimore, Maryland, to conduct conference business, which included the announcement of the ministerial appointments for the next year. Morgan College, "the third black Methodist Episcopal school organized in 1866" for the purpose of educating the freed slaves,[2] often served as the meeting place for black Methodists of the Washington Conference.

Annual conference was more than just several days of business meetings. It was, in fact, a special time of spiritual renewal for the participants. Morning and evening sessions often began with someone leading the group in a hymn such as "Where He Leads Me," by E. W. Blandy and John Samuel Norris, or "Stand by Me," by Charles Albert Tindley—who was one of Philadelphia's noted black Methodist preachers.[3] Following the song leader, the audience would pick up the tune and begin to sway as the harmonic sounds filled the air.

Later many would sense the presence of the Holy Spirit as they listened intently to the sermonized biblical stories, passionately and vividly told by one of the noted black preachers, whose voice would rise in a crescendo, backed by the echoing sounds of "Thank you, Lawd" and "Amen, Brother!" Following the worship service and business session, conference attendees gathered on the campus grounds to eat their favorite foods picnic style and enjoy the fellowship with friends and colleagues, many of whom they had not seen since the last annual meeting.

The 1920 conference was particularly special and held historic significance for the black Methodists of the Washington Conference. Bishop Matthew Wesley Clair, Sr., had recently been elected a bishop and was presiding over the Washington Annual Conference. Bishop Clair was one of the first two African American Methodist bishops elected to the episcopacy, the other being Bishop Robert E. Jones.[4] Prior to their election, the four Methodist Episcopal missionary bishops who had been elected previously—Francis Burns (1858), John W. Roberts (1866), Isaiah B. Scott (1904), and Alexander P. Camphor (1916)—were limited to service in Liberia, West Africa.[5]

Bishop Clair, noted for his eloquent preaching, was well known to the delegates at Morgan. He was a member of their conference, had pastored Asbury Methodist Episcopal Church in Washington, D.C., and prior to his election as bishop, had served as a supervising pastor, or district superintendent, of the Washington District.

The conference was a particularly special event for the Reverend David DeWitt Turpeau and his wife, Ila Marshall Turpeau. Bishop Clair, a good friend, had agreed to baptize their three-month-old daughter, Leontine, the seventh of their living children. On June 6, at Mount Zion Methodist Episcopal Church of Georgetown in Washington, D.C., which was pastored by Mr. Turpeau, Bishop

Clair performed the baptismal ceremony of Leontine Ruth.[6] The baby was named after her father's sister, Leonee, and Ruth Mosley, the daughter of George and Annie Mosley (who had become surrogate parents to David Turpeau when he moved to Mount Kisco, New York, from Louisiana). According to family narratives, Bishop Clair uttered the words: *Oh, how I wish you were a boy so that my mantle might fall upon you.*

Certainly, he could not have imagined that his wish, which was intended for a male child, would actually be realized sixty years later. Neither her parents nor her siblings—Anita Bell, David Dewitt, Woodruff, DeWolf Rossman, Angella Felonise, Florida Marshall, or Michel Martine—could have imagined that Leontine, nicknamed "Teenie," would achieve such heights. Women preachers were an anomaly in those days. It would not be until 1926, when Leontine was six years old, that the first African American woman, the Reverend Laura J. Lange of the Lexington Conference of the Methodist Episcopal Church, would be ordained a deacon and later, in 1936, an elder by Bishop Clair.[7] But "God moves in mysterious ways, His wonders to perform,"[8] and history would later record that Leontine Ruth Turpeau Current Kelly was the first African American woman bishop to be elected in The United Methodist Church, or any mainline denomination in the world.

CHAPTER TWO

A Firm Foundation

Leontine's father, David DeWitt Turpeau, Sr., was born of creole parents in St. Martinsville, Louisiana, in 1874—eleven years after President Abraham Lincoln signed the Emancipation Proclamation, which "freed all slaves except those in states or parts of states that were not in rebellion." The Civil War had ended, and the political, economic, and social reconstruction of the South was at its height. In 1873, seven African Americans had been elected to the forty-third Congress: Robert B. Elliot, R. H. Cain, A. J. Ransier, J. H. Rainey, of South Carolina; James T. Rapier of Alabama; J. T. Walls of Florida; and John R. Lynch of Mississippi. In 1874, Blanche K. Bruce, an African American from Mississippi, was elected to the Senate.[1] Though David's father was Roman Catholic and his eight children were baptized in the Roman Catholic Church, David took an interesting journey into the ministry of the Methodist Episcopal Church. It began with his meeting D. Frank Dakin of Mount Kisco, New York, at Gilbert Academy in 1892.

In America during the 1890s, an increasing number of blacks, then called Negroes, were graduating from secondary schools and colleges. These educational institutions, including Gilbert Academy, had been established for freed slaves by religious denominations and the federal government in the late 1860s and 1870s. Many of the graduates owned farms, belonged to labor unions, or were trained physicians, journalists, lawyers, politicians, and clergymen.[2] Yet, this was also a period of rising hostilities toward blacks. The lynching of black males increased throughout the decade in the South, and disenfranchisement of blacks through intimidation, violence, poll tax requirements, and other complicated balloting processes were helping eliminate the many gains made by blacks during Reconstruction.

David Turpeau was in his late teens when he left St. Martinsville and traveled to Baldwin, Louisiana (also known as Winstead), to visit his sisters, Carrie, Angella, and Maggie Turpeau. They were enrolled at the Methodist Freedmen's Aid Society's Gilbert Academy, which was later known as New Orleans University. During the visit, David met and befriended D. Frank Dakin, who had been serving as the instructor of carpentry for three years and was supervising the building of the campus chapel.[3]

David remained with his sisters until the following spring, when he left Louisiana with Dakin to seek other employment opportunities and traveled three days by train to New York via the Illinois Central Railroad. He arrived at the New Castle-Kisco Depot on March 9, 1893. The village of Mount Kisco was nestled along the east bank of the Hudson River, thirty-seven miles from New York City, and had an estimated population of fifteen hundred, which included the only African Americans in town: Mr. and Mrs. George L. Mosley.[4] The landscape of this quiet, sleepy New England village with its trees, flowers, streams, and wooded hills was totally unlike the swamps, cypress, and Louisiana bayous where David had grown up.

D. Frank Dakin brought "little David," as he was affectionately called by the Dakin family, to the home of his parents, James and Rosalie Dakin: a stately Victorian-style, three-story house, with a wraparound covered porch that overlooked Dakin Avenue. David was provided with his own room in the attic and had a place at the table with Frank and his brothers: Clarence, Raymond, Ernest, and Harvey.[5]

The Dakin family, active members of Mount Kisco Methodist Episcopal Church, owned Dakin's Sash and Blind Factory and Dakin Construction Company. They took a special interest in David and provided him with a job in the factory. They were also instrumental in his receiving a college education. This unique opportunity occurred when Mrs. Dakin attended a meeting where she heard the outstanding Reverend M. C. B. Mason, field secretary for the Freedmen's Aid and Southern Education Society of the Methodist Episcopal Church, talk about providing black students with a college education at the schools established by the Society for freed slaves. The Reverend Mason was the first African American to hold a staff position in the Methodist Episcopal Church and served as field secretary and, later, as corresponding secretary for the Freedmen's Aid and Southern Education Society.[6] When Mrs. Dakin returned home, she was determined to have David complete high school as quickly as possible and go to college. Upon his graduation from Mount Kisco High School in 1896, the Dakins, with support from Mount Kisco Methodist Episcopal Church, where David had become a full member in 1894, sent him to Bennett College in Greensboro, North Carolina.[7] He received his Bachelor of Science degree in 1899.

Although thirty-eight years had passed since slavery had ended, David knew that returning to Louisiana was out of the question. At the beginning of the twentieth century, racism toward blacks continued to be overt. "In the last sixteen years of the nineteenth century there had been more than 2,500 lynchings, the great majority of which were of African Americans, with Mississippi, Alabama, Georgia, and Louisiana leading the nation."[8] On the train back to Mount Kisco following his graduation from Bennett College, David met a black Methodist minister, the Reverend C. M. Chase, who was on his way to the Delaware Conference of the Methodist Episcopal Church in Milford, Delaware. Their conversations influenced David to consider the ministry as a vocation, and David accompanied Mr. Chase to the conference. Mr. Chase recommended to Bishop Cyrous D. Forst that David be ordained because he had just received his college degree. David, however, did not have a seminary degree, so the Bishop appointed him as a "supply" pastor in Ossining, New York. In 1900 David enrolled in Drew Seminary in Madison, New Jersey, became a full member of the Delaware Conference, was appointed to John Wesley Methodist Episcopal Church in New Haven, Connecticut, and took summer classes at Yale University Divinity School. David's sisters introduced him, by correspondence, to one of their classmates at New Orleans University, Ila Marshall of New Orleans. On November 3, 1901, David and Ila were married by the Reverend I. L. Thomas, pastor of Asbury Methodist Episcopal Church, Washington, D.C.[9]

Since Ila and David had never seen each other prior to their wedding, they agreed that, for identification purposes, they would both wear a red rose in their lapel when they arrived at the Washington, D.C., train station. David, at age twenty-eight, had long been an immaculate and stylish dresser, and because of his profession, he was expected to wear formal dress suits at all times. This special day was no exception. He was dressed in his best Edwardian high buttoned cutaway frock coat, pants, vest with pocket watch, high collar shirt, bow tie, and bowler hat when, walking down Union Station's platform, he saw an eighteen-year-old, "tall blond with blue eyes and sandy long straight hair."[10] A red rose was pinned to the lapel of the traveling coat she wore that covered the high collared, puffed-sleeved blouse of her turn-of-the-century shirtwaist dress.

David immediately recognized that Ila, though of black ancestry, was a product of miscegenation and could have easily been mistaken for a white woman. He also knew that it would not matter to some in the train station that he was an educated black man whose grand-father had migrated to Louisiana from the French colony St. Martinique as a freedman in the mid 1800s. He and Ila both knew instinctively that David's life could be in danger because of the societal practice of accusing black men of rape and lynching them if they were seen talking directly to or appearing to have an intimate conversation with a white woman. Ila was just as concerned for her own well-being. Since childhood, she had endured many racial slurs and hostile comments from whites, as well as blacks, because of the color of her skin. Sensing the potential danger but recognizing the red rose, David walked past Ila, turned, and, without uttering a sound, picked up her luggage and followed her out of the train station. It was not until they were inside his car-riage that they felt it was safe to speak to one another as they drove to meet the Reverend Thomas for their wedding.

A year later, David received his Bachelor of Divinity degree from Drew Seminary and was assigned to Hud-son, New York. On July 4, the first of ten children, Anita Bell Mosley Turpeau, was born. A few weeks later the Reverend Frederick Carpenter, then pastor of Mount Kisco Methodist Episcopal Church, baptized Anita at George and Annie (affectionately called Mam and Pap by David) Mosley's Mount Kisco home.[11]

By the turn of the century, Methodists were heavily involved with many of the social and political changes occurring in the country. Many church leaders were strong supporters of the National Prohibition Party, Women's Christian Temperance Union, and the National Anti-Saloon League.[12] The strong drive to outlaw alcohol even resulted in Methodists replacing wine at their communion services. Political activity on social issues increased and led to the establishment of the Board of Temperance in 1904 and the Federation for Social Service in 1907,[13] and to the passage of the Social Creed of Methodism in 1908.[14]

David became actively involved with the temperance movement when he joined the staff of the Colored Department of the Maryland State Anti-Saloon League in 1915. The temperance committee for the Washington Conference later recognized his work with the League during its fifty-second session:

> "We record with profound thanksgiving our high appreciation of the splendid work for and in behalf of the Anti-Saloon League which has *been done among our race during the past two years by the Rev. D. DeWitt Turpeau.*"[15]

At the time of Leontine's birth on March 5, 1920, in what was known as the "O Street Parsonage" (2902 O Street, NW), David and Ila had been pastoring a growing congregation at Mount Zion Methodist Episcopal Church for four years. Their oldest, Anita, had completed Dunbar High School and was enrolled at Howard University.

Mount Zion, the oldest African American congregation in the District of Columbia, was founded in 1816 and located in historic Georgetown. The Georgetown community was a microcosm of the northern and midwestern cities of the United States. American industrialization, including the growth of factories and steel mills, was in full bloom. The migration of African Americans from the South to the North and Midwest, along with the influx of European immigrants was affecting the social, political, and economic conditions of persons living in northern cities.[16]

The National Association for the Advancement of Colored People (NAACP) and The National Urban League had been founded, and the number of black fraternal organizations, unions, newspapers, businesses, and college-educated blacks was on the rise. The woman suffrage movement had succeeded in getting the Nineteenth Amendment passed, which gave women the right to vote.[17] Booker T. Washington, W. E. B. Du Bois, James Weldon Johnson, and Marcus Garvey were among the intellectual and political voices of the black community that were raising the nation's consciousness about and proposing solutions to the issues of racism, segregation, and economic oppression of blacks in the United States.

Georgetown, classified in 1920 as "industrial" by city ordinance, had a mixture of black and white residents who were federal employees, small businessmen (for example, restaurateurs, barbers, tailors, beauticians), professionals (doctors and pharmacists), semi-skilled laborers, and persons with other occupations.[18] Many African American blue- and white-collar workers were members of Mount Zion. David capitalized on their talents and skills by involving them in creative fund-raising activities such as church-wide pageants, which were often coordinated by Ila; annual men's rallies; women's, boys', and girls' day programs. A motivating instrument, created by David and used to inspire his members, was a weekly newsletter, *The Mount Zion Herald,* which was edited by the pastor and publicized the church's fund-raising accomplishments and forthcoming events.

At the fifty-seventh session of the Washington Conference, Bishop Matthew Clair, Sr., appointed David to complete Clair's term as district superintendent of the Washington District, which Clair vacated when he became bishop. David served for four years as the superintendent for the Washington District. During this period the last of Ila and David's eight surviving children was born in 1923. Michel "Mickey" Martine Turpeau carried the full name of his paternal great-grandfather and grandfather.

In 1924 David, called "Papa" by his children, was appointed to Warren Methodist Episcopal Church in Pittsburgh. Two years later, Teenie enrolled at Watts Elementary School in Pittsburgh, following behind her sisters Florida ("Toots") and Angella ("Gella"). DeWitt, Jr. ("Dee"), began classes at the University of Pittsburgh; Woodruff ("Wood") enrolled in printing classes at Ralston High School; and Rossman ("Raw") was in his last year of grammar school.

In the spring of 1927, Teenie and her favorite brother, Mickey, had an interesting encounter with one of Methodism's outstanding church leaders of the era, the Reverend Dr. Gloster Robert Bryant. It was a period of transition for Dr. Bryant, who had recently been transferred from Calvary Methodist Episcopal Church in Cincinnati, in the Lexington Conference, and appointed to Warren Methodist Episcopal Church in Pittsburgh, in the Washington Conference. At Ila's insistence, Dr. Bryant stayed with the Turpeau family at the parsonage. The children, having heard their parents talk about the numerous contributions Dr. Bryant had made within the church, were in awe of this aristocratic, six foot, dark-skinned man, who dressed in "swallowtail" suits with vests and "Prince Albert" shirts.[19]

Dr. Bryant, ordained an elder in the West Texas Conference in 1893,[20] was recognized as a noted orator as well as the founder and builder of Methodist Episcopal churches in Texas, Los Angeles, and Pasadena, California (1892–1910). After transferring from the Southern California Conference to the Lexington Conference, he pastored churches in Kentucky, Indiana, Illinois, Michigan, and Ohio and served as a district superintendent in the Lexington Conference for eleven years.[21] In Chicago, Dr. Bryant pastored South Park Avenue Methodist Episcopal Church (now Hartzell Memorial United Methodist Church), and in 1919, established the Hartzell Social and Industrial Center. Named for Bishop Joseph Crane Hartzell, the Center provided a variety of skilled training classes for blacks migrating from the South. Dr. Bryant, also active on the national church level, served as a reserve delegate to the 1916, 1920, and 1924 General Conferences of the Methodist Episcopal Church, which were held in Saratoga, New York; Des Moines, Iowa; and Springfield, Massachusetts, respectively.[22]

In 1924, Dr. Bryant was transferred to Park Street Methodist Episcopal Church in Cincinnati. Within his first year, he succeeded in purchasing the "famous old St. Paul Church" from the white Methodists. On Sunday, November 22, 1925, Dr. Bryant moved the black congregation of Park Street Church into the huge gothic structure that once housed St. Paul. The church's name was changed to Calvary Methodist Episcopal Church.[23] In addition to the acquisition of the church building, the purchase included a sixteen-room parsonage, a day care for children of working mothers, and a home for single working women, which was supported by the Women's Home Missionary Society. Unfortunately, Dr. Bryant did not reap the benefits of his vision. When the annual meeting of the Lexington conference ended, church politics resulted in his appointment and transfer to Pittsburgh. This appointment was a traumatic blow for Dr. Bryant, and it resulted in his eventual withdrawal, in 1929, from the denomination that he loved so dearly.

Teenie recalls that one day, while Dr. Bryant was residing at the Turpeau parsonage in Pittsburgh, she and Mickey were sitting at the bottom of the steps listening to Dr. Bryant's oratorical voice preaching a sermon. They watched as Dr. Bryant left his bedroom and went into the bathroom, his voice still booming from the bedroom. They were stunned by what appeared to be a magical act. Later they learned that Dr. Bryant, who was known for his fascination with modern gadgets, had recorded his sermon on a new American invention, the Dictaphone.

As a child, Teenie was unaware of the political and emotional implications the transfer, or "pulpit swapping," of Dr. Bryant to Warren Methodist Episcopal Church in Pittsburgh and her father's appointment to Calvary Methodist Episcopal Church in Cincinnati would have on the Turpeau and Bryant families in the years to come. However, her childhood encounter with Dr. Bryant would represent just one of the many threads woven into the tapestry of Leontine's life.

CHAPTER THREE

Calvary

Cincinnati was the home of the Turpeaus during the presidential tenures of Calvin Coolidge (1923–1929) and Herbert C. Hoover (1929–1933). Teenie, Florida, and Mickey enrolled at Harriet Beecher Stowe School; and Angella and Rossman transferred to Old Woodward High School. Teenie's eldest sister, Anita, had already graduated cum laude from Howard University and married scholar Thomas Jefferson (T. J.) Anderson, Sr. Anita was a teacher, and T. J. served as principal of the James Adams School in Coatsville, Pennsylvania. Teenie's oldest brother, DeWitt, had completed Pittsburgh University and was enrolled at Drew Seminary. After finishing Drew, he would follow his father and be ordained in the Lexington Conference of the Methodist Episcopal Church along with his friend Matthew Wesley Clair, Jr., whose father baptized Teenie. Matthew, Jr., would follow in his father's footsteps as well and be elected to the episcopacy in 1952.

During David's seven-year pastorate at Calvary in downtown Cincinnati, the church served as one of the major educational, social, and political centers in the black community. Calvary's congregation grew to more than eight hundred members and was ranked as one of the largest churches in the Lexington Conference, along-side St. Mark in Chicago and Union Memorial in St.

Louis. Though Christian in its beliefs and doctrine, Calvary, like most black churches regardless of denomination, expressed its Christianity in distinctly different ways than its white counterparts. For example, songs, musical arrangements, the mode of worship, and preaching styles incorporated African and African American cultural forms of expression. The church community was as an integral part of its members' daily lives, facilitating the spiritual, educational, social, political, and, to some degree, economic support needed to survive in American society. Thus Calvary, like its sister churches, served as "the central institutional sector in black communities," providing its members with a shared Afro-Christian religious worldview and faith perspective.[1]

As "preacher's kids," the Turpeau children were actively involved in many church activities. Ila Turpeau, called "Mama" by her children, organized talent programs and pageants involving the childen, youth, and adults of the church. One major church event was a religious drama, written and directed by Ila, entitled "Comrades of the Cross." This story of Christ, told through hymns and narration, involved over one hundred members of Calvary Church. Leontine was three years old the first time she appeared in one of Mama's annual mass productions, and she continued to participate through her high school years.

One of Teenie's childhood recollections of her participation in church activities was an event that often occured during revivals or after one of Papa's sermons. In the order of service, following the sermon and in response to the preached word, Papa or the visiting minister would "open the doors of the church," officially known as giving the Invitation to Christian Discipleship. Persons were invited to claim their belief in Jesus Christ and if they did not belong to a church community, to affiliate with Calvary and its members. After the minister's invitation, Teenie would always respond and go to the altar to join. This would happen whether anyone else came to the altar in response to the preached Word or not. She did it so regularly that it became a family joke with members admonishing her to remain in her seat. Nevertheless, several years passed before she ceased her automatic response to the invitation. In addition to her own activities, Teenie recalls that her brothers, Rossman and Woodruff, were active members of the church's "Gilpin Dramatic Club," which involved many of the church's teenagers and young adults in staged performances during Calvary's anniversary celebrations.

These two brothers were also responsible for discovering what Teenie would later call the "true ministry of Calvary": the ministry that occurred in the 1800s when Calvary was Union Chapel Methodist Episcopal—prior to being renamed St. Paul Methodist Episcopal Church.[2] "One day Woodruff and I were crawling under the basement of the church and ran into a trap door," recalled Rossman. Seeing a brick-layered passage, they lured their baby sister into it to determine how deep it was. "We then got candles and crawled into it,"[3] he remembered. When the boys told their father about their discovery, David took them next door to the basement of the parsonage where they discovered the other section of the passageway. It was clear to Papa Turpeau, as he shared historical events with the family gathered for dinner around the large mahogany, oval-shaped table, that the hidden passage was probably part of the Underground Railroad and that Calvary Church, when occupied by white Methodists during slavery, may have been one of its stations.[4]

Years later in her high school library, Teenie came across a map that displayed a series of stations for the Underground Railroad, including Calvary's parsonage and a Jewish synagogue. Calvary was one of two Methodist churches pastored by David Turpeau that had a history of supporting the anti-slavery movement. Historical church records of Mount Zion Methodist Episcopal Church in Washington, D.C., document that the church also "served as one of the stations in the Underground Railroad, and the vault in the nearby Old Methodist Burying Ground was used as a hideout for runaway slaves until their passage North could be arranged."[5]

As was the case with most families during this period in American history, the home was the center of the educational, moral, and spiritual development of the Turpeau children. For black families who daily faced the frustrations and indignities of living in a racially segregated society each day, home, church, school, community, and fraternal organizations were the major institutions that influenced the values and mores of the family members regardless of their age. These institutions enabled thousands of African Americans to enhance their personal growth, develop and demonstrate their creative talents, hold leadership positions, establish and operate organizations to benefit the black community, and develop and sustain black entrepreneurship.

Although most households had radios and the movie industry was becoming a powerful influence on Americans,[6] family games played around the dining room table (such as checkers or charades) and talent shows held in the parlor were a major source of entertainment in the Turpeau household. Florida, or Anita if she was visiting, would play the piano, and family members would gather to sing Papa and Mama's favorite hymns or popular tunes of the day. Everyone, regardless of age, learned a scripture verse, song, or poem that would be shared when his or her turn came. All would listen as their mother recited her favorite Paul Lawrence Dunbar poems, such as "When de Co'n Pone's Hot," "When Malindy Sings," or "In the Morning." Like many church families, the Turpeaus were also expected to perform at Sunday afternoon teas. In addition, when David and Ila traveled to white churches in the area to promote race relations the younger children went along to perform special programs—often written by their mother.

Like most households, the dining room table was more than just a place for meals. It served as the place where Mama and Papa not only taught appropriate table manners but encouraged their children to develop their conversational skills. Family discussions usually focused on local and national events, church politics, the social and economic concerns of the community, and the celebration of any achievements made by blacks. Since segregation required that visiting black educators, lay and clergy church officials, and civil rights leaders stay in peoples' homes rather than in hotels, the Turpeau parsonage often included traveling dignitaries.

Leontine recalled several visits by one of Papa's best friends, the Reverend W. A. C. Hughes (1877–1940), "director of the influential Department of Negro Work, Board of Missions and Church Extension" and "later elected to the episcopacy . . . in 1940."[7] Another regular visitor was the outstanding preacher and pastor of St. Mark Church, New York, the Reverend Lorenzo Houston King (1878–1946). Elected editor of the *Southwestern Christian Advocate* at the 1920 General Conference (serving in that position until 1931), King articulated the issues and rights of Negroes and was recognized as a national religious leader. Mr. King ran unsuccessfully for Congress in 1938 but was elected to the episcopacy in the Methodist Church in 1940.[8] Another friend who often visited the Turpeau home was the Reverend J. W. Golden (1883–1961), a member of the Negro Fraternal Council of Churches (1934–1965) and father of Charles Franklin Golden (1912–1984), who was elected to the episcopacy in 1960.[9]

One influential person who left an indelible impression on young Teenie was the famous Mary McLeod Bethune. In 1923, Mrs. Bethune became the first woman president of a Methodist Episcopal college and the first woman founder-president "to head the merged Cookman Institute and Daytona Industrial School for Girls," later renamed Bethune-Cookman College, which is located in Daytona Beach, Florida. She also founded the National Council of Negro Women, represented the Methodist Church to the Federal Council of Churches for forty-one years, and served on the executive committee of the Federal Council of Churches.[10]

Perhaps Mrs. Bethune and Ila had developed a relationship because Ila was an active leader with the YWCA, serving on its board of directors and as its president; because Ila was one of the founders of the local Urban League affiliate; or because David and Ila were active leaders in the community and the NAACP and were involved with the Republican Party. Whatever the foundation, the reason for this particular visit was that Mrs. Bethune had been in Cincinnati to meet with James N. Gamble, noted manufacturer and philanthropist.

Mr. Gamble served as the president of the Board of Trustees of the Daytona Normal and Industrial Institute and spearheaded, with the Board of Education for Negroes of the Methodist Episcopal Church, the institute's merger with Cookman Institute of Jacksonville, Florida.[11] After her meeting, Mrs. Bethune stopped by the parsonage to visit with Ila. Leontine opened the front door, and Mrs. Bethune said, "Well, young lady, what do you plan to do with your life?" She was so awestruck with Mrs. Bethune's overwhelming and powerful presence that she could not open her mouth. Yet, she remembered Mrs. Bethune's question and her distinctive personality.

Active in the community, David and Ila encouraged their children to do likewise. One of the house rules was that a group could not be joined unless a public service component was an integral part of the organization. This meant no bridge or dance clubs! One of Calvary Church's members, called "Mother Townes" by the parishioners, began an organization for girls ages seven to twelve. "Mother Townes's Sewing Circle" became one of Teenie's first organizations. Later, she joined Florida and Angella and became active with the Young Women's Christian Association's (YWCA) girls program, while Mickey was active with Boy Scouts and the YMCA.

The early 1930s found America experiencing the worst depression in its history. Along with high unemployment, business failures increased, banks closed, mines shut down, farmers lost their property, and black as well as white workers lost their jobs. "Within a few years after the beginning of the Great Depression millions of American citizens were regarded as incapable of self-support in any occupation. By 1934, for example, 17 percent of whites and 38 percent of blacks were placed in this category."[12]

The Hoover Administration and the Republican Party failed to provide direct relief to the increasing number of hungry and homeless Americans. To oppose Hoover in the upcoming election, the Democrats selected New York Governor Franklin Delano Roosevelt as their presidential candidate. Roosevelt "had pioneered a model relief program and . . . had engineered other social programs such as old-age pensions, unemployment insurance, and public power programs."[13] In November 1932, Franklin D. Roosevelt was elected President of the United States.

During his first one hundred days in office, Roosevelt introduced sweeping legislation, titled the New Deal, that addressed the national emergency by establishing the Federal Deposit Insurance Corporation, the Home Owners Loan Corporation, the Federal Securities Act, and job programs like the Civilian Conservation Corps. In 1936, he was reelected in a landslide victory and launched a "Second New Deal" to attack the Great Depression.[14]

Since the period of Reconstruction, blacks had aligned themselves with the Republican Party, and it was not easy for them to switch allegiance in 1932. However, President Roosevelt was not long in office before he gained a large following among African Americans in response to his New Deal programs. Mrs. Eleanor Roosevelt, who was greatly admired by African Americans and known to be a friend of Mary McLeod Bethune, was a public advocate for programs and projects that addressed problems faced by African Americans. These and other factors led to a major shift of political alliance from the Republican Party by blacks to the party of Roosevelt.[15]

As devastating as the Depression was, David Turpeau, by God's grace, found the means to ensure that his children received a college education. By the time Teenie began high school at Old Woodward High, her sisters Angella and Florida were both in college. Angella received her Bachelor of Arts degree from Howard University in 1935, and Florida received her degree from Bennett College in 1937. Bennett College, Papa's alma mater, had been reorganized as a liberal arts college for African American women in 1926.

DeWitt, after pastoring at Butler Methodist Episcopal Church in Evanston, Illinois, and then moving to Centenary Methodist Episcopal Church in Akron, Ohio, received a Master of Arts degree from the University of Akron, was awarded an honorary degree from Philander Smith College in Little Rock, Arkansas,[16] and married Corinne Cloud of Cincinnati on August 21, 1935. Woodruff became a member of the Typographical Union of Ohio, worked for the *Chicago Defender Newspaper,* and later joined the faculty of Philander Smith College teaching printing and journalism. Rossman initially attended Clark College in Atlanta then transferred to West Virginia State College, a land grant college that had been established for the education of blacks in 1891.

By Teenie's senior year she was an active member of the YWCA's Girl Reserves and was elected the first black president of the Greater Cincinnati Girl Reserves, which included Northern Kentucky. An incident related to her election and reflective of the racist attitudes that blacks encountered regularly in Cincinnati occurred shortly after her election.

Unlike the schools across the river in Kentucky and other southern states, Cincinnati public schools had desegregated when Teenie was in high school. However, she and her classmates were still victims of racist school policies and procedures that were initiated by school officials. On one occasion, the principal of Woodward High School announced, in a called assembly, that no "Negro" would stand on the auditorium's stage as long as he was principal. It was believed that this policy was created because a black student was to be named valedictorian for that year, a first for Woodward, and the principal was not going to allow him on the stage. In the interim, the YWCA's Greater Cincinnati Girl Reserve had planned a major meeting to be held at the high school and this policy had a direct effect upon the new president's ability to preside over the sessions. After YWCA leaders threatened to take the issue to the school board, the policy was revoked, and Teenie did in fact stand on that stage!

Another school policy allowed black students to use the high school swimming pool only at the end of the day on Fridays before the pool was drained for the weekend. Prior to coming to Woodward High School, Leontine had become a licensed lifeguard and a member of the girl's aquatics team at Stowe School. When she transferred to Woodward, the white girls took gym on Tuesdays and swimming on Thursdays. The black girls took gym on Tuesdays and Thursdays but were not allowed to take swimming, though they could swim on Fridays after school closed. School officials' rationale for this policy was that the "oil in the black girls' hair" clogged the pool.

Although somewhat accustomed to being excluded from the proms held at private "whites only" country clubs and the extracurricular activities sponsored by the school, Teenie and her friends were active with the junior NAACP and were constantly reminded by members of the black community and its institutions of their value and worth as children of God. They were taught black history and could name the black educational, political, and cultural leaders of their day; they had their proms and social activities at the Colored Women's club in Walnut Hills; and they were instilled with a sense of racial pride and the belief that regardless of the color of their skin, they could succeed in society and the world. Armed with the support of their parents and community, Teenie and her friends were involved in one of Cincinnati's first sit-ins, which occurred after one of the high school football games.

Teenie and six of her friends went to a restaurant located in downtown Cincinnati at Fountain Square, a place frequented by the students. According to Teenie, the waitress refused to wait on them and told them to leave the premises. They refused, and when the manager came to the table, he told the waitress to serve them but to break their plates. They were served, and as they left they witnessed the waitress breaking their plates.

The next week they returned with twenty students, ordered their food, were served, and watched the waitress break the plates again. The following Friday when they came to the restaurant, the manager directed the waitress to serve them—but not to break the plates!

CHAPTER FOUR

Unification

As the 1930s drew to a close, the Methodist Episcopal Church, the Methodist Protestants, and the Methodist Episcopal Church, South, had renewed discussions on reunification and finalized plans that were originally developed by a Joint Commission on Unification in 1919.[1] A Joint Commission of the three branches convened on August 27-29, 1934, in Chicago. There were two additional meetings of the Joint Commission, in Louisville, Kentucky, on March 13-14, 1935, and in Evanston, Illinois, on August 14-16, 1938.[2] The three churches finally merged on May 10, 1939.

Race, a dominant focus in American society since the institution of slavery, was a constant issue among Methodists. Moreover, Methodist history reflects an interesting and continuing ambivalence regarding the matter. Historical records document the involvement of African Americans in the early Methodist societies in America: slaves were evangelized by Methodists, and many noted black Methodist preachers converted whites and blacks—one of whom, Harry Hosier, was converted by Bishop Francis Asbury.[3] It had been the issue of slavery that had dominated the 1844 General Conference, resulting in the separation of the Methodist Episcopal Church and the formation of the Methodist Episcopal Church, South. Segregation of the races was also the

dominant issue in the unification of the two denominational bodies, and the creation of a Central Jurisdiction
was devised as a solution to their differences. The Central Jurisdiction concentrated approximately 375,000
black Methodists into a single region. The pros and cons
of this segregated structure would be debated throughout the remaining years of the twentieth century, even
after a second major denominational merger that began
in 1964 and ended with the formation of The United
Methodist Church in 1968.[4]

The nineteen black conferences of the Methodist Episcopal Church were represented in the negotiations, which
eventually led to the 1939 merger, by two black delegates:
I. Garland Penn and Robert E. Jones.[5] "The new plan
called for the formation of 'The Methodist Church.' It
would have one general conference and six jurisdictional
conferences, five of them geographical, the sixth for the
Negro annual conferences. Equal representation was provided for ministers and lay persons in all conference levels. The office of bishop would continue to be organized
in a Council of Bishops, . . . [and a] Judicial Council would
act as supreme arbiter of the law of the church."[6] Jurisdictions would control regional affairs, the election of bishops, and "promote the evangelistic, educational,
missionary, and benevolent interests of the Church." The
episcopacy would become localized, meaning that a General Conference would no longer elect the bishops, and
except in special cases, bishops were to live and govern
within the jurisdiction they were elected in.[7]

In the Turpeau household during Teenie's high school
years, there were many conversations around the dinner
table that focused on the positive and negative ramifica-
tions of the proposed merger and a racially segregated
Central Jurisdiction of black Methodists. This was a time
in American history when African Americans were pushing against the boundaries of segregation and second-

class citizenship and were seeking a more inclusive society. Ila and David were strong supporters of the Urban League and NAACP movements and actively involved in local politics. Anita, then living in Washington, D.C., where her husband taught at Howard University, was actively involved with Mary McLeod Bethune's efforts to establish the National Council of Negro Women.[8]

The unification plan created strong reactions and concerns among the majority of black Methodists, and Teenie recalled DeWitt, who was pastoring Mt. Pleasant Methodist Episcopal Church in Cleveland, Ohio, then transferred to Indiana Avenue (Gorham United Methodist Church) in Chicago in 1937, often talked with Papa about the denomination's plan to legally structure a racially exclusive jurisdiction.

James S. Thomas noted:

> The Plan of Union had been adopted by a large margin of positive votes in the General Conferences of the Methodist Episcopal Church, the Methodist Protestant Church, and the Methodist Episcopal Church, South. . . .
> Of the forty-seven African American delegates to the General Conference, thirty-six voted against the Plan of Union and eleven abstained.[9]

Dr. James P. Brawley, president of Clark College and delegate to the Uniting Conference expressed the feelings of most African American Methodists:

> It was the hope of the Negro membership of the Methodist Episcopal Church that this status would be improved in the new united church and that no structural organization would set him apart and give him less dignity and recognition than he already had. . . .
> He, therefore, rejected the plan of union. . . . This was a stigma too humiliating to accept.[10]

Because of the Methodist Episcopal Church's historic stand against slavery and for the establishment of schools for freed slaves, the belief in providing educational access to all persons, and the commitment to social justice, David chose not to withdraw from the Methodist Episcopal Church when it united with the Methodist Episcopal Church, South. He felt that black Methodists must battle for inclusiveness from within and continue to hold the Church accountable to the gospel of Jesus Christ. When the merger occurred in 1939, David was not alone in this position. Dr. Major J. Jones, former president and dean of Methodist-affiliated Gammon Theological Seminary, writing on black Methodists' reasons for not leaving the denomination when it established the Central Jurisdiction, said:

> Black people had been a part of the Methodist movement since its inception in America and did not intend to withdraw or separate themselves from their religious heritage and history. Second, most of them were economically related to the church, and to withdraw from the Methodist Episcopal Church was to withdraw from their support. Third, there were many who felt that they could better address the issues of separation from within the church than from outside it. Fourth, there were many who reasoned that even though it would be divided constitutionally by race, there would still be broader leadership opportunities available within the new structure than were available in the church prior to Union.[11]

Methodist church historian Dr. Karen Collier wrote, "Negroes repudiated the plan. The 1936 Methodist Episcopal Church General Conference voted 470 to 83 in favor of the plan. Negro delegates represented a substantial part of the opposition, with 36 voting decisive nos and 11 abstaining. . . . In Annual Conferences, seven of the nineteen Negro Annual Conferences voted against the plan. Of the remaining twelve, some voted favorably, and some refused to vote. . . . The final plan was totally unacceptable to a majority of Negro Methodists."[12] Collier further stated that "Negro members of the Methodist Episcopal Church affirmed the creation of a new church on the basis that they would continue within the mainstream of the predominantly white structure. . . . The plan was reinterpreted to reflect their racial pride—recognizing a degree of independence without being a part of a caste system or without being thrust out of the church."[13]

Three years prior to the Uniting Conference, at the 1936 meeting of the Lexington Annual Conference, as black Methodists discussed the pros and cons of the plans for merger, David was appointed district superintendent of the Lexington District, and his friend Bishop Matthew W. Clair, Sr., retired. Bishop Clair's retirement created a vacancy in the episcopal leadership, and at the 1936 General Conference, Willis J. King, then president of Gammon Theological Seminary; W. A. C. Hughes, director of the Department of Negro Work, Board of Missions and Church Extension; and Alexander P. Shaw, editor of the *Southwestern Christian Advocate*, were nominated as candidates to fill the position. Alexander P. Shaw, recognized as an outstanding preacher, pastor, and administrator was elected. W. A. C. Hughes (1940) and Willis J. King (1944) were later elected to the episcopacy. That same year, David was recruited by the Republican Organization of Hamilton County and ran unsuccessfully for the Ohio State General Assembly.

Also in 1936, Dr. Gloster Robert Bryant died of tuberculosis in Pittsburgh—disappointed and disillusioned with the Methodist Episcopal Church after several efforts to sustain a congregation of Christian believers. One of these attempts was his Emmanuel People's Church, founded in 1929 and housed in the Royal Circle of Friends hall at Fifty-first and Michigan Boulevard in Chicago; sadly, it floundered and failed during the Depression.[14] Dr. Bryant returned to Pittsburgh in 1931, and over the next five years, while he battled blindness and ill health due to diabetes, he established Emmanuel Church and Emmanuel College, an interdenominational Christian education and music school.

On December 28, 1936, in a joint ceremony performed by Papa, Angella married Dr. Raymond Hayes of Indianapolis, and Rossman married Christine Boone of Newport News, Virginia.

After graduation from Woodward High School in 1937, Leontine enrolled at the University of Cincinnati but transferred to West Virginia State College in 1938. Also that year, her father was successfully elected, by a twenty-five thousand majority vote, to the Ohio State General Assembly House of Representatives. Later, he was elected to three consecutive terms and served on the House of Representatives Finance, Public Welfare, and Federal Relations Committee. Simultaneously, David also served five years as district superintendent for the Lexington District.

Teenie and Mickey were the last to leave for college. Leontine, though not a shy person but somewhat sheltered and naive, became one of the "adopted daughters" of Mrs. Anne Brock, who was serving as the dormitory director of McCorkle Hall at West Virginia State College at the time. Mrs. Brock's youngest daughter, Anne (named after her mother), became one of Teenie's best friends, and when Mickey came to West Virginia State College in 1940, he and Anne fell in love and were married after World War II in 1946. Teenie became actively involved in the college chapter of the NAACP and was initiated into Alpha Kappa Alpha sorority, the oldest African American women's Greek organization—founded at Howard University in 1909.

During her sophomore year, a young jazz musician and sophomore at Detroit Institute of Technology in Detroit, who had his own band called The Nightingales, was recruited by West Virginia State College president, Dr. John W. Davis, to help organize the college orchestra. Gloster Bryant Current, son of Earsey and John T. Current and eldest grandchild of Dr. Gloster Robert Bryant, arrived on the campus of West Virginia State College in the fall of 1939, with members of his Nightingales who desired a college education. This young man's presence on the campus of West Virginia State College became another major thread in the weaving of Leontine's life journey.

Prior to coming to West Virginia State College, Gloster, called "GBC" by his classmates, had been an active organizer of NAACP youth councils in Detroit. Inspired by National NAACP youth director, Juanita E. Jackson, who had addressed the youth council members at a September 6, 1936, meeting at Scott Methodist Church, GBC became a key leader in the planning and coordination of the 1937 youth section of the NAACP's twenty-eighth annual conference. (Juanita Jackson later married Clarence Mitchell, who would become one of the nation's noted civil rights leaders.) The annual conference met in Detroit, June 29–July 4, 1937. Following the convention, the youth councils pushed for job opportunities, sponsored a debate team, and participated in the local branches' membership drive for one thousand new members.[15]

Theester "Sippie" Coleman, the business manager of West Virginia State College, confirmed the president's offer for GBC and his band to come to the college and indicated that Dr. Davis wanted them to play at the convention, known as the Boulé, of the most private, exclusive, and prestigious fraternal organization Sigma Pi Phi that was scheduled for that July at the college.[16] In the interim, Detroit branch NAACP president, Dr. James J. McClendon, and treasurer, Mrs. Mamie L. Thompson, offered GBC the newly established branch position as executive secretary. When he could not accept their offer, they agreed to hold the position until he completed his college education.

After arriving at West Virginia State College, GBC recruited additional college students with musical talent and organized the West Virginia Collegians during his first week on campus; by that Saturday they were ready to play their first dance on the campus. The band became popular throughout the state. In addition to the band, GBC organized an orchestra in which he exhibited his skills playing the xylophone as well as the saxophone. GBC, who came to campus as a member of Kappa Alpha Psi fraternity, was elected Polemarch of Tau Chapter within a year and served on the debate team.

As college life began to provide Teenie, GBC, and their classmates opportunities for leadership and for educational and personal growth through its various campus organizations, Hitler's armies marched into Poland. England and France declared war on Germany and World War II began; Italy, under the leadership of Mussolini, had already invaded Ethiopia and formed an alliance with Adolph Hitler called the Rome-Berlin Axis; and Japan was at war with China.

American public opinion was divided over the nation's foreign policy, but most people believed it was inevitable that America would be drawn into a war with Germany and Italy. Thousands of African American college students began to face the reality that they too would be called into service. Despite America's Jim Crow laws, their status as second-class citizens, and previous experiences in segregated armed forces, many believed that democracy, as opposed to socialism and communism, was the best form of government and that the barriers of racial discrimination would eventually be destroyed.

The 1940 Selective Service Act was amended with a clause forbidding discrimination in the drafting and training of men; however, discrimination in the armed forces and segregation of black units continued. Political pressure from black leaders, including Walter White of the NAACP and A. Philip Randolph, then president of the National Negro Congress and the Brotherhood of Sleeping Car Porters, resulted in some black appointments and promotions. Colonel B. O. Davis became the first black brigadier general, William H. Hastie was appointed civilian aide to the secretary of war, and Colonel Campbell Johnson became executive assistant to the director of Selective Service. Senior Reserve Officer Training Corps (ROTC) units were added at West Virginia State College, Hampton Institute, North Carolina Agricultural and Technical College, Prairie View State College, and Tuskegee Institute, and three million African Americans registered with the armed forces.[17]

As Americans began to prepare for war, the Methodist Church was beginning to experience the results of the May 10, 1939, Kansas City, Missouri, Uniting Conference and the creation of the Central Jurisdiction. Following the first General Conference of The Methodist Church in April 1940, the first Central Jurisdictional Conference convened in June at Union Memorial Methodist Church in St. Louis. Its major task was the election of bishops. W. A. C. Hughes, then secretary of Colored Work of the Board of Home Missions and Church Extension, was the first bishop to be elected and assigned to the New Orleans Area. The second bishop to be elected was Lorenzo Houston King, pastor of St. Mark's Church in New York City and former editor of the *Southwestern Christian Advocate*. He was assigned to the Atlantic Coast Area, which encompassed Georgia, Florida, Alabama, and South Carolina. The remaining bishops were Robert E. Jones, elected in 1920 and assigned to the Columbus

(Ohio) Area, and Bishop Alexander P. Shaw, elected in 1936 and assigned to the Baltimore Area, which included the area from New York and New Jersey south to North Carolina and west through Tennessee.[18]

During this time, David was completing his fourth year as district superintendent. He served on the bishop's cabinet with Bishop Alexander P. Shaw for one year and with Bishop Robert E. Jones for two years. As they prepared for the first meeting of the Central Jurisdiction, David and Ila Turpeau hosted the last meeting of the Lexington Conference, under the structure that existed prior to the formation of the Central Jurisdiction on April 12, 1939, in Cincinnati.[19]

Meanwhile, following an NAACP student conference held at Virginia Union University in March 1940, GBC, Teenie, and the two hundred members of the West Virginia State College NAACP chapter organized and hosted the second student conference that fall. Delegates from twenty-two colleges and universities attended, and noted educators, civil rights leaders, attorneys, and legislators participated in the program. Lincoln University delegate, Roy C. Nichols, was also in attendance.[20] Years later, in July 1968, Roy Nichols would become the first black bishop to be elected in the new United Methodist Church.[21] At this historic student conference in 1940, the officers elected were: James T. Wright (Howard University) as president, James Ramsey (Paine College) as first vice president, Leontine Turpeau (West Virginia State College) as second vice president, and Earl David (West Virginia State College) as publicist.

Love blossomed between Teenie and GBC, and they became engaged. In June 1941, in order to graduate, GBC sold his xylophone and pawned his portable typewriter to pay the outstanding fees, but it was not enough. Reflecting upon his college years, GBC recalled: "My parents were so poor they could not even come to college to see me march. When I walked across the stage, . . . I was given a 'dummy' diploma," understanding that the real diploma would not be received until the bill was paid.[22] About a month later, GBC received his real diploma, and he has always believed Sippie Coleman in the college's business office had taken care of his outstanding balance.

On July 15, Gloster became the first executive secretary of the Detroit branch of the NAACP, and on September 6, 1941, he and Leontine were married at the Turpeau home at 1566 John Street, Cincinnati. Florida, who had married Randall Hudson Anderson, Sr., in 1938 stood with her as matron of honor.

The dynamics of growing up in a large family affect children in different ways. There was a seventeen-year spread between Teenie and her oldest sister, Anita, and when Teenie became a young woman, it was Anita who became her role model and a major influence upon her spiritual growth and development. Although Teenie was the baby girl, Mickey, three years younger, was doted on by their mother from the day of his birth through his early years at college. Teenie's maternal nurturing and affirmation, therefore, came from her older siblings who were still at home or from extended family members. It is unclear how or when the phrase "poor Teenie," which was often repeated by her mother, began. The words, however, affected her self-esteem and several years passed before she overcame their effect on her sense of self. Teenie's relationship with and understanding of her mother developed more substantially during her middle adult years when her mother lived with her and when Teenie began evolving into a more secure and confident person.

Papa Turpeau, like most men of that era, was not only viewed as the head of the household but as the disciplinarian. As a pastor and politician, he was popular and compassionate with the public and his congregants, yet at home, he often displayed a somewhat distant persona to the younger children. It was not until the summers during her college years, when she served as her father's secretary, that Leontine began to gain better insight into her father's personality and an appreciation for his vocation and avocation.

CHAPTER FIVE

New Paths

After moving to Detroit in 1941, Teenie joined Second Grace Methodist Church, where her husband's parents, Earsey and John T. Current, affectionately called "Mother and Daddy," attended with their children: Lester, Isabelle, Gloria, John, Jr. ("Johnny"), and Delores ("Dee Dee").

Earsey, daughter of Dr. Gloster R. and Texanna Bryant, met John T. when Dr. Bryant pastored in Kentucky. In 1912, Earsey and John T. married after Dr. Bryant transferred to Indianapolis, and they moved with Dr. Bryant when he relocated to Chicago to serve as district superintendent for the Chicago-Indianapolis district. When Dr. Bryant was appointed to Scott Methodist Episcopal Church in Detroit in 1923, Earsey, John T., and their first set of children—Gloster, Lester, and Isabelle—also relocated from Chicago to Detroit and became members of Scott Church. John T., trained in gold-plating and watchmaking, opened a watch repair shop with a shoe repairman and rented a house on Twelfth and Trumbull Streets, near the baseball stadium. Just before Gloria was born, John T. rented a larger house on Detroit's west side. It was on the west side of Detroit that John T. eventually purchased the family homestead at 6526 Beechwood Street.

While pastoring Scott Church, Dr. Bryant, noted for sending members from the congregation to establish mission churches in other parts of a city, organized Second Grace on the west side of Detroit, St. Paul Methodist Episcopal Church in the Eight Mile Road-Wyoming area, and Emmanuel Mission on Detroit's east side.[1] After Dr. Bryant was appointed to Park Street (Calvary) in Cincinnati in 1924, the Current family transferred its membership to Second Grace Methodist Episcopal Church.

Second Grace, under the pastoral leadership of the Reverend Alvin Burton, held its services in a two-family flat at 6435 Ironwood Street until 1950. With funds raised by the congregation and John T. Current, who mortgaged his home, along with the Methodist Union and the Lexington Conference, a permanent home for the church was purchased from the Whitefield Methodist Church on Tireman Road.[2]

John T. and Earsey Current were sustained by their faith in God as they struggled to provide for their family. Their spiritual resilience, their willingness to proclaim the gospel of Jesus Christ and witness to others about God's grace and mercy, gave them a mutual respect for others. When the Current children were young, the family would perform musical programs. Earsey played the piano; John played the violin; GBC played the sax, piano, and xylophone; and Lester played the trumpet. Isabelle, a naturally born artist, would sketch whatever she was inspired to draw. Teenie remembered that they were well known for their musical talent and appeared at churches throughout the Lexington Conference.

Active laypersons in their local church and organizations within the Lexington Conference, John T. served several years on the Conference Board of Church Location and, in 1950, was the first African American to become a trustee of the Methodist Union of Greater Detroit.[3] Earsey, a leader and officer in the Women's Society of Christian Service, often saw Ila during the summers at the annual Women's Society of Christian Service Schools of Mission meeting. This unique organization of black Methodist women from local churches throughout the Central Jurisdiction was organized just prior to the ratification of the Plan of Union and became "an integral part of the origin, formation, growth, and development of the Women's Division of Christian Service."[4]

Teenie and GBC had been married just three months when the Japanese, intent on conquering Asia despite opposition to such aggression by the United States, launched a surprise attack on Pearl Harbor in Hawaii on December 7, 1941. The bombing damaged submarines, ships, and planes and almost destroyed the United States Pacific fleet. The following day, Congress passed a resolution authorizing a state of war with Japan. Three days later, in response to Germany and Italy's declaration of war against the United States, Congress voted unanimously to enter a state of war against Germany and Italy.

Thousands of black workers migrated from the South to Detroit and other parts of the Midwest in search of employment in the defense industry as the war began to escalate. Numerous discrimination complaints were lodged with the NAACP, where Gloster was immersed in his work: initiating, coordinating, and implementing strategies with other civil rights workers to eradicate discrimination in the work place, labor unions, automobile industry, housing industry, and the armed forces. By June 1942, his efforts had resulted in the Detroit branch's membership growing to 11,119, the largest number of members in any one city.[5]

As the country and its people felt the effect of these local and national events in a variety of ways, Teenie, who had promised her father that she would finish her college education, enrolled at Wayne State College. According to her recollections, however, she was more enthralled with being Mrs. GBC, preferring to learn new recipes rather than study her college textbooks. Fate intervened, and before long, she and GBC were expecting. On August 13, 1942, I was born.

The black-owned *Michigan Chronicle* and the *Detroit Tribune* announced my birth and whether I would be named "Angella Patricia" according to my mother's intentions or "Sojourner Truth" after the great abolition-ist as announced by my father. The *Detroit Tribune*, Sat-urday August 22, 1942, stated:

> Adding another member to the Detroit NAACP, Mrs. Leontine Turpeau Current, wife of the executive sec-retary gave birth to a baby girl Aug. 13, at Parkside Hospital. Although the baby will be christened "Angella Patricia," the father vows that the newcom-er will be nicknamed "Sojourner Truth" in honor of the great abolitionist.[6]

Perhaps the real reason for suggesting the name of Sojourner Truth was directly related to a major civil rights battle in Detroit at the time. The Sojourner Truth Citizens Committee and the Detroit NAACP branch had combined their efforts in an endeavor to force the Detroit Housing Commission to reverse its decision to house white workers in the two hundred Sojourner Truth homes, which had been originally designated for black workers. The issue gained national attention and resulted in the Housing Commission reversing its decision and permitting blacks to occupy the Sojourner Truth homes.[7]

While Gloster engaged members of the NAACP in the branch's efforts to break down barriers of discrimination and advance the economic and political rights of first-class citizenship status for Detroit's blacks, Leontine's time was spent caring for the new baby. Like many mothers, she started a scrapbook, which included pho-tographs of great-grandparents, grandparents, and other relatives, newspaper clippings, and letters from various cousins. She also included several pages of notes and commentaries that she felt would enhance her child's sense of self, family connectedness, and relationships.

The year 1946 brought new life and new beginnings. Americans had inaugurated Franklin D. Roosevelt for an unprecedented fourth term the previous year. Within six months they mourned his death, and Vice President Harry S. Truman became the nation's thirty-third president. World War II, which had put more than thirteen million Americans into uniform,[8] finally ended after the invasion of Europe by the Allied Forces and the dropping of atomic bombs on Hiroshima and Nagasaki, Japan.[9]

Teenie returned home to Cincinnati to deliver her second child on January 8, 1946. He was named Gloster Bryant, Jr. A few months later, while Papa Turpeau was attending a meeting of the Lexington Conference in Detroit, Gloster Jr. and his cousin Marian Lynn Turpeau, who was the daughter of Teenie's brother, Woodruff, and her sister-in-law, Marian, were baptized in a joint service conducted by "Grandpa" Turpeau and the Reverend Alvin Burton at Second Grace Methodist Episcopal Church.

Soon after that event, Gloster, having succeeded in establishing the NAACP's largest branch by increasing its membership from six thousand in 1941 to twenty-five thousand in 1946, was recognized by NAACP leaders at the national office and appointed national youth director by Walter White, president of the NAACP. This event precipitated the family's move to New York City. Within that same year, Gloster was promoted to director of branches for the national organization.

The move to New York was filled with new and exciting opportunities, but it also held emotional setbacks. New York was a long way from family members. As Gloster began to establish new NAACP branches around the United States, his work required travel away from home. Teenie was left to adapt to a new environment and care for two young children without the cadre of family or friends who had provided an important support system for her in the past.

In Jamaica, Long Island, where Gloster and Teenie found an apartment, there was only one black Methodist Episcopal church. Accustomed to regular church attendance and the black worship experience, the family affiliated with Brooks Memorial Methodist Church though it was not in close proximity to their neighborhood. "In the black church going to church is more than attending a worship service. It is a way of gathering all of what the people are; the event brings the spiritual response of the community to the experience of suffering. Going to church offers a way of deciphering the meaning of living life in relation to God and neighbor. It is a time to reflect and to provide ways the human spirit can transcend the multifarious conditions of racial oppression. . . . It is a time for celebrating survival and freedom and renewing hope."[10] Many Sunday mornings, in search of spiritual inspiration and renewal, Teenie would walk approximately two miles to Brooks Church while pushing Gloster, Jr., in the baby carriage with me in tow.

In 1947, the Reverend James David Kelly was appointed by Bishop Edward Wendell Kelly to establish a second predominantly black Methodist church in Jamaica. Teenie and Gloster, Sr., became charter members of St. Paul Methodist Church, and both were actively involved in the church's membership development and building program. St. Paul became the home church for Gloster, Sr., who served in the succeeding years as St. Paul's assistant pastor, minister of music, director of the youth choir, organist, and in various other leadership capacities until his death in 1997.

Nineteen forty-seven was a difficult year for Leontine. On February 13, Grandpa Turpeau died of a cerebral hemorrhage at the age of seventy-three. He was in his fifth term as a state representative from Hamilton County, Ohio. The funeral was held at Mount Zion Methodist Church in the Walnut Hills area of Cincinnati, where the members of the Turpeau family who had remained in Cincinnati had transferred their membership. Grandpa's death was a major loss for the family, and Ila Turpeau became the family matriarch. During the next six years a variety of factors created emotional stress and strain that began affecting Leontine and GBC's marriage and undermining the family's stability.

As millions of Americans were readjusting to life after World War II, increasing numbers of African Americans who had fought in the war were pressuring local and federal governments to change their treatment of African Americans. During the initial days of the Cold War Era, the NAACP and other organizations began to press for full equality. Gloster, Sr., now a vital member of the NAACP leadership team as the director of branches and field administration, and his colleagues Walter White, Roy Wilkins, Clarence Mitchell, Thurgood Marshall, and Henry Moon began traveling throughout the country expanding the NAACP's operations by increasing its membership and number of branches and filing more legal suits to obtain the right to vote, desegregate schools, and acquire other civil rights for African Americans.

Similar pressure was being mounted by black and white leaders, who were challenging the justification for continuing the Central Jurisdiction within The Methodist Church. They continued to remind the Church that the plan creating the Central Jurisdiction "was never approved by a majority of the Negro membership, and it was not considered to be a final solution to the racial issue" within the denomination.[11]

In the midst of his professional organizational activity within the NAACP and his volunteer service in church, Gloster, Sr., obtained his Master's in Public Administration in 1951 from Wayne State University in Detroit. His active involvement at St. Paul Methodist Church led to a desire to pursue his call to use his gifts in service and ministry for God, and with the support of the Reverend Kelly, Gloster was ordained a deacon by Bishop Edgar A. Love at the 1953 Delaware Annual Conference, which met at Tindley Temple in Philadelphia.

Bishop Love, former superintendent of the Department of Negro Work for the Board of Missions, was elected (along with Bishop Matthew W. Clair, Jr.) to the episcopacy at the 1952 Fourth Central Jurisdictional Conference held at Tindley Temple Methodist Church in Philadelphia and was assigned to the Baltimore area, which included the Delaware Annual Conference. Also during the 1952 meeting, continuing concern regarding the segregated structure of the Central Jurisdiction was discussed. Dr. James P. Brawley, the president of Clark College in Atlanta, presented the report of the Commission to Study the Central Jurisdiction and later succeeded in passing his proposal that the College of Bishops of the Central Jurisdiction, two ministers and two laymen from each area of the Jurisdiction, serve on the continuing Commission.[12]

As Gloster's job responsibilities and travel schedule increased, his attention to Teenie's needs for companionship and emotional support waned. Although he may have felt that their marriage would last forever and their relationship was stable—they had acquired a house and car, had an income that provided the basic necessities, and had children who were well cared for and loved—for Teenie it proved not to be enough. She began to experience illness and depression and, already slight of build, started to lose weight. The weight loss resulted in a kidney disorder, which required her to wear a steel belt to hold her kidneys up and in place when she stood.

When Teenie became pregnant in 1953, she began to gain weight; however, her doctor was concerned about her ablility to carry the baby to full term and decided that for her final two months she needed complete bed rest. It was decided that when the school year ended, Teenie, Gloster

Jr., and I would go to Cincinnati to live with her sister Florida and Hudson, Florida's husband. The household also included Ila, who was called "Nana" by the grandchildren, and their sons Hudson, Jr., David, Jimmy, and Michel. Gloster, Sr., arranged visits to Cincinnati between NAACP branch meetings and NAACP Legal Defense Fund activities. On September 5, John David, named for his two grandfathers, was born. Unhappy in her marriage, Teenie decided not to return to New York and enrolled Gloster, Jr., and me in elementary school in Cincinnati.

With GBC in New York and Teenie and the children in Cincinnati, it became clear that Teenie had become somewhat of a single parent. When she filed for and received a divorce in 1955, an uncommon and to some degree socially unacceptable practice at the time, she decided to seek employment to supplement the child support payments and develop her self-esteem.

Though Teenie had secretarial skills, she had not completed her college education and employment options were limited. In addition, it was important to her that her work hours coincide with the children's school day, so for a year she sold Avon products. Later, she applied for a secretarial position with the Cincinnati Public School system. Before she could interview with the five schools that had job openings, God opened another door of opportunity, and she was offered the position of director of children's activities at Fellowship House, which was modeled after the well-known Fellowship House in Philadelphia. Several leaders in Cincinnati, after visiting the Fellowship House in Philadelphia, decided to establish a meeting space for the purpose of improving race relations. By fostering interaction among persons of different races, religious faiths, cultures, and economic backgrounds through activities and dialogue, it was their hope that community understanding and relationships would improve.

Cincinnati's Fellowship House was located on Highland Avenue within an "Appalachian" community composed of a large number of whites with low incomes who had migrated from Tennessee and Kentucky. Fellowship House sponsored programs that allowed interfaith and interracial leaders throughout the city to engage one another and area residents in dialogue on social and racial issues in an effort to improve their understanding of one another and to encourage a greater sense of community among people.

Marion Spencer, a board member of Fellowship House, political leader, and family friend, approached Teenie about developing a children's program on racial understanding utilizing one hundred handcrafted interracial dolls from around the world. The dolls, which were given to the House by a female World War II Jewish refugee, were replicas of famous people, such as Albert Einstein (scientist), Mary McLeod Bethune (educator), and Marian Anderson (contralto). Leontine developed the program using the dolls to express to children and adults her Christian understanding of inclusiveness and her belief that human beings are God's children regardless of the color of their skin, their religious background, or their economic class. She conducted the program regularly at Fellowship House, for children in scout troops across the city, and in local churches when invited. The salary from this position enabled Teenie and the children to move into their own apartment.

Although only a block away from Nana, Florida, Hudson, and the children, the move to the Ruth Street apartment was significant in many ways. First, it was a freeing experience for Teenie and the children. They now had their own private living space and could be a family unit without the stress inherent in living in someone else's house no matter how supportive, caring, or uninterfering that person may be. Second, it symbolized the steps Teenie was taking toward self-sufficiency and independence. She was defying the "poor Teenie" nickname she had been saddled with since childhood. Adhering to the words found in Hebrews 10:23, "Let us hold unswervingly to the hope we profess, for he who promised is faithful"(NIV), she stepped out on faith, demonstrating her belief and trust that God would provide a way for her to have a fulfilling life.

DAVID AND ILA TURPEAU AND FAMILY (1923)

Left to right, back row: Woodruff, Anita, Rossman; Front row:
Leontine on lap of David D. Turpeau, Sr., Florida, Michel Martine'
(Mickey) on the lap of Ila M. Turpeau, DeWitt, Angella.
Georgetown, Washington, D.C.

DAVID DEWITT TURPEAU, SR. (1900-1902)

Archives of Mt. Kisco United Methodist Church,
Mt. Kisco, NY.

GLOSTER ROBERT BRYANT (1916-1923)

District Superintendent, Chicago-Indianapolis, Lexington
Conference; Pastor, South Park Methodist Episcopal Church,
1918–1923.

MT. ZION UNITED METHODIST CHURCH

Historic Landmark, Georgetown, Washington, D.C.

MT. ZION UNITED METHODIST CHURCH,
THE FIRST BLACK METHODIST CHURCH
IN WASHINGTON, D.C.
FOUNDED OCTOBER 16 1816
IS DESIGNATED A DISTRICT OF COLUMBIA
HISTORIC LANDMARK.
IT WAS LISTED IN THE NATIONAL REGISTER
OF HISTORIC PLACES ON JULY 24 1975

MT. ZION UNITED METHODIST CHURCH PARSONAGE

Birthplace of Bishop Kelly.

FAMILY PHOTO (1934)

Reverend David DeWitt and Ila Turpeau family, Cincinnati, Ohio.
Back row, left to right: Leontine, Florida, Rossman, Woodruff,
DeWitt, Angella, Anita; Front row: Ila, Michel, David DeWitt, Sr.

BAPTISM OF GLOSTER BRYANT CURRENT, JR. AND MARION LYNN TURPEAU (1946)

Second Grace Methodist Episcopal Church, Detroit, Mich., 1946. First row, left to right: Earsey Current, Marion Lynn Turpeau held by David DeWitt Turpeau, Sr., Gloster B. Current, Jr., held by John T. Current, Sr., Catherine Hill; Second row, left to right: Woodruff Turpeau, Marion Turpeau, Gloster B. Current, Sr., Leontine, two unknown, Charles Tweed Parker, Mrs. Lucille Graves, Attorney William Graves.

REV. LEONTINE KELLY (1970)

Left to right: Ila M. Turpeau (mother), Leontine, Anita T. Anderson (sister). Galilee United Methodist Church, Edwardsville, VA.

EPISCOPAL CONSECRATION (1984)

Western Jurisdictional Conference Consecration of Bishops, July 20,
1984. Center, left to right, Bishops: Jack Tuell, W. Kenneth Goodson,
Calvin McConnell; Far right front: Reverend Barbara Troxell; Left,
front to back: Reverend Diedra Kriewald; Bishops: Marvin Stuart,
Melvin Talbert, Nathaniel Linsey.

REV. GLOSTER B. CURRENT, SR. (1983)

Westchester United Methodist Church, Bronx, NY. Left to right:
Gloster B. Current, pastor, Bishop Roy C. Nichols.

FAMILY PHOTO (2000)

Left to right, back row: Leon, John David, Pam, Gloster; Second row: John D. Jr., Faith, Staci, Yvonne, Tiffany, Angelyn; Front row: Angella, Leontine, July 2000.

BISHOP KELLY (1999)

Bishop Leontine Turpeau Current Kelly (age 79).

CHAPTER SIX

Standing on God's Promises

In 1953, at the NAACP's forty-fourth Annual Convention, Dr. Chánning H. Tobias called for "Freedom in America by '63" in his keynote address. This launched the "Free by '63 Campaign," and the ten-year goal to eliminate all forms of state-imposed racial discrimination captivated blacks throughout the country.[1]

By 1954, the NAACP and its team of brilliant lawyers—Thurgood Marshall (later to become the first African American appointed to the Supreme Court), Robert L. Carter, Jack Greenberg, Louis Redding, James Nabrit, George E. C. Hayes, Spottswood Robinson III, and others—successfully won a series of legal cases eroding the Supreme Court's 1896 separate-but-equal doctrine. Segregationists in all the southern states actively resisted the Supreme Court's 1954 landmark decision in *Brown v. Board of Education of Topeka*, which ruled that school segregation was unconstitutional.[2]

It was during these turbulent times that Bishop Edgar A. Love transferred the Reverend James David Kelly from St. Paul Methodist Church in Jamaica, New York, to East Vine Street Methodist Church in Knoxville. Before this transfer, David had successfully established St. Paul Methodist Church, and with the technical assistance of the Reverend Dennis R. Fletcher from the Board of Missions, Section on Church Extension, the congregation had acquired property and built a new church facility.

Prior to David's transition, Dr. Dewitt Dykes, Sr., district superintendent for the Knoxville District of the East Tennessee Conference, accepted a position at the Board of Missions. Subsequently, in addition to being appointed to East Vine Street Methodist Church, the bishop also appointed David Kelly to complete Dr. Dykes's term. Under David's leadership, East Vine Street purchased a new building, merged with Seney Chapel, and was renamed Lennon-Seney Methodist Church.

As district superintendent, David attended several church conferences in Cincinnati and, during one of these meetings, visited with Leontine and her children. In 1956, David and Leontine were married, and she and the children relocated to Knoxville. The following year, Gloster, Sr., married Rebecca Eleanor Busch of Indianapolis. Rebecca was also from a family of active Methodists. Her grandparents, Paul and Mary Phifer, were members of Scott Church in Detroit; her stepfather, the Reverend Squire Braxton Lester, an ordained elder in the Lexington Conference, pastored several churches and served as a district superintendent in Indiana. Her mother, Maridelle Estelle Phifer Busch Lester, was actively involved with the Women's Society of Christian Service. Rebecca's exposure to the mission programs supported by the Women's Society of Christian Service inspired her, after graduate study, to become part of the US-2 (the Board of Mission's two year domestic missionary program), serving in Little Rock.

After moving to Knoxville, Leontine, who was encouraged by David to pursue her college course work in order to receive an undergraduate degree, enrolled at Knoxville College. John David was three; Gloster, Jr., eleven, was enrolled in elementary school and later joined me at Vine Junior High School.

Living in Tennessee exposed us to the policies of segregation for the first time. Vine Junior was the first segregated school we had ever attended, having lived in New York and Cincinnati where public schools were integrated. Our experience, however, proved positive, for though there were limited educational resources and facilities, Gloster Jr., and I found the principal, staff, and teachers (who were all African American) to be attentive, supportive, and committed to helping us achieve academic success—attributes and attitudes that we had not previously experienced as minority students in northern schools.

I established peer relationships and became active in Vine Junior's extracurricular activities. A highlight of the next year was being elected, along with another classmate, to represent the junior high school in the "Youth Appreciation Week" parade sponsored by Optimist International. Just before school closed for the summer, Gloster, Jr., and I were informed that the family was moving to Richmond, Virginia. The announcement was not well received; to me, a budding adolescent with a growing group of teenage friends, moving seemed like a major disruption to my life.

The move was precipitated by a call from Bishop Edgar Love. A few weeks before the school term ended, Bishop Love advised David that Leigh Street Methodist Episcopal Church in Richmond had an opening for a ministerial appointment. The city government was planning to revitalize the area in which the church was located and the congregation needed a minister who could assist them in moving to a new facility. David's ministerial strengths were establishing new congregations, building churches, and helping congregations relocate.

Leigh Street Methodist Church sat on the corner of Fifth and Leigh Streets in downtown Richmond. Its parsonage, a white frame house located directly behind the church at 501 Fifth Street, was stately when built in the early 1920s, but by 1958 it had lost its glamour. The house was a great contrast to the East Vine Street (Lennon-Seney) Church's parsonage. The four-bedroom house in Knoxville, with its modernized kitchen, breakfast nook, beautiful living and dining rooms, and sun porch, sat on Morningside Drive and was surrounded by dogwood, cherry, and oak trees. The Leigh Street house on Fifth Street had no backyard and only a little patch of grass in the front that separated the crumbling red brick sidewalks from the steps leading to the front porch. Mama often reminded us to appreciate having a roof over our heads, that the church members were sacrificing to provide the pastor's family with a decent place to live.

Ministers who serve in denominations that provide housing for the pastors and their families have varied experiences with church parsonages. Although the style, location, and furnishings differ from church to church, a congregation's size and median income often give little indication about the appearance or condition of the parsonage. Leigh Street prided itself on being a vital African American middle class church; though, unlike East Vine Street, it only had a few children and youth. The congregation was composed of school teachers, small business owners, a few unskilled laborers, domestic workers, and community leaders. One member of the congregation was a young lawyer named Willard Douglas, who became a member of the Judiciary Council of The United Methodist Church in 1984. Today, Judge Douglas credits the prophetic witness of David and Leontine Kelly and their leadership for helping him achieve many firsts in the Virginia annual conference and the General Church. Judge Douglas recalls that David Kelly's persistence that Douglas become involved in conference activities, resulted in Douglas's serving as the first African American layman elected to the General and Jurisdictional Conferences in 1972.

Another member of Leigh Street was Dr. Nathaniel Lee, the church organist and choir director. Though he later became assistant superintendent of the Richmond public schools, during this time, he was my high school choir director and loved by many of his students. In those days, the sanctuary choir did not sing gospel music but performed a wide range of anthems, and Dr. Lee knew how to capitalize on the melodious voices of the few young adults in the choir, and their harmony would make the anthems resonate throughout the sanctuary.

Directly opposite the church was the neighborhood tavern, and on Saturday nights, people who imbibed too much alcohol would talk loudly to themselves as they swayed and stumbled past the parsonage. Sometimes, while David and Teenie were at evening church services, Gloster, Jr., and I would hide under the upstairs window and, using his slingshot, practice aiming spit balls or pebbles at these "wayward souls." One night we almost got caught! Several prestigious churches and businesses were also located in the community. Just a half block from the parsonage was one of Richmond's largest black churches, Fifth Street Baptist Church. The Phyllis Wheatley YWCA and the YMCA were three blocks away. Eggleston's, the hotel for blacks, was located on Second Street near the The Hippodrome, one of the "for blacks only" theaters. The other theater, The Walker Theater—located on Broad Street—was in walking distance, but several blocks away from the parsonage. Six blocks away from the parsonage was the home of the renowned Maggie L. Walker. Walker was a noted entrepreneur, the president of Richmond's Consolidated Bank and Trust Company, a member of the Richmond Council of Negro Women, and a supporter of education from the 1920s through the 1940s. At one time, Richmond's downtown area had been part of a thriving business and residential community; however, thirty years later, it was showing signs of neighborhood deterioration and urban blight.

I enrolled at Maggie L. Walker High School, Gloster, Jr., attended Graves Jr. High School, John David was not old enough for Navy Hill Elementary School but was enrolled a year later, and Mama, determined to obtain her B.A. degree in history and sociology before her daughter graduated from high school, transferred her Knoxville College credits and enrolled at Virginia Union University. She graduated from Virginia Union with honors in 1960.

During the summers, Gloster, Jr., and I spent a few weeks in Detroit with our paternal grandparents, affectionately called "Mother and Daddy Current," and the remaining weeks with our father in Hollis Long Island, New York. On Sundays in Detroit we attended worship services at Second Grace Methodist Church, sitting with Mother Current on the family's unofficial pew (the third row from the front, to the left of the pulpit) and observing our aunts and uncles singing in the choir. Daddy Current always sat at the front on the right side of the pulpit and would remain after church for hours counting every penny of the offering receipts—paying the pastor's salary first, then the other church expenses. Regardless of how hungry we were, neither the grandchildren nor the other members of the family could devour Mother Current's "melt in your mouth" rolls, fried chicken, mashed potatoes, or delicious peach cobbler until Daddy Current returned home from church.

When we were in New York, Gloster, Jr., and I worked in Dad's office at the NAACP national headquarters, where we were exposed daily to the civil rights and religious leaders actively involved in the struggle for equality. Until we were old enough to obtain real employment, we stapled membership cards, cleaned a huge map of the United States, placed pins on the map where NAACP branches were located, and ran errands for NAACP staffers Lucille

Black, membership secretary, and Bobbie Branch, office manager. We also attended the NAACP annual conventions witnessing the organization's tributes to persons such as Rosa Parks, who was the NAACP's Montgomery Branch secretary, and Martin L. King—both of whom were honored at the fiftieth Convention for their roles in the Montgomery, Alabama, bus boycott. In addition, we became accustomed to conversational exchanges with such notable personalities as Medgar Evers, Thurgood Marshall, Clarence and Juanita Jackson Mitchell, Henry Moon, and Roy Wilkins.

As the decade of the historical and turbulent 1960s approached, African American students grew tired of living with segregation in the South: having to use separate bathroom facilities, drinking from segregated water fountains, being prohibited from eating in public restaurants, attending segregated movie houses, riding past white schools to attend black schools in southern cities that refused to adhere to the Supreme Court's famous May 17, 1954, decision—and hundreds of other indignities. As a result, these students were rebelling against their parents en masse. They no longer cared about the admonitions from their parents and community leaders to be careful and not openly confront the segregated institutions and policies of discrimination in America.

The college students at Virginia Union University organized a student protest movement in Richmond and conducted sit-ins at the lunch counters and stores on Broad Street. In the midst of the growing racial tensions in Richmond during the fall of 1960, Leontine joined the faculty at Armstrong High School, one of the segregated black high schools, to teach social studies and economics.

While at Armstrong, she and fellow teachers, from both Maggie Walker and Armstrong High Schools, were conscious of the changes occurring in society and the importance of preparing their students to confront the challenges of a desegregated society. Just as Leontine had constantly assured her own children that they were loved by God and were precious in God's sight, regardless of the color of their skin, she spread the same message to her students at Armstrong as she prepared them for higher academic pursuits. The students were affirmed and assured that they could be successful in life despite the "separate but unequal" school system. They were constantly reminded by their teachers that new opportunities for blacks were on the horizon. Walkerites, including Arthur Ashe (the first black Wimbledon tennis champion) and Isaiah Jackson (internationally renowned classical conductor), Armstrongites, including Maxie C. Robinson, Jr. (the first African American major television network anchorman) and Maxie's brother Randall Robinson (founder of TransAfrica), were just a few of the success stories of that era.

During the summer months when school was out, Leontine completed the required courses and obtained her certified lay speaker's license. She also enrolled and took graduate courses in economics and history at North Texas State University and later at the University of Cincinnati.

By the spring of 1963, thousands of students throughout the South, white and black, were being arrested for trespassing, disorderly conduct, and disobeying police officers as they attempted to force desegregation of public facilities. Many black churches—of all denominations, in the North and the South—were becoming sanctuaries for mass meetings and strategic planning sessions for local NAACP branches, the Student Non-Violent Coordinating Committee, the Southern Christian Leadership Conference, and others.

Simultaneously, The Methodist Church, with more than 350,000 African American members, was being pushed by black church leaders and others to address the issue of a racially segregated denomination. Though the 1960 General Conference debated and adopted the report of the Commission to Study and Recommend

Action Concerning the Jurisdictional System, along with its recommendations to increase racial understanding, no proposal to change the racially segregated Central Jurisdiction was presented.

The sixth session of the Central Jurisdictional Conference (which opened July 13, 1960, in Cleveland, Ohio), however, authorized a committee of five persons, one from each Episcopal area, "to work in conjunction with the jurisdictional Committee on Christian Social Concerns and the representatives of the Commission on Inter-Jurisdictional Relations" to do a study of the Central Jurisdiction and "give special attention to the methods and procedures by which the Central Jurisdiction may be dissolved."[3] Members of that committee were: Richard C. Erwin of the Baltimore Area, the Reverend John H. Graham of the Nashville-Birmingham Area (staff member of the General Board of Missions), William Astor Kirk of the New Orleans Area (staff member of the General Board of Christian Social Concerns), and the Reverend John J. Hicks of the St. Louis Area (pastor of Union Memorial Church); the Reverend James S. Thomas of the Atlantic Coast Area (staff member of the General Board of Education) served as its chair.[4]

Concurrent with the general church's resistance to confronting the issue of a racially segregated church and society, Thelma Stevens, executive secretary of the Department of Christian Social Relations and Local Church Activities who was often called a "Crusader for Racial Justice,"[5] was working to bring racial harmony to the Church. Stevens and many other white Methodist women were actively involved in laying the groundwork among Methodist women for a Christian understanding of the principles of nonviolence and for support of the desegregation of schools through a national Conference on Human Relations, which was cosponsored by the Women's Division and the Board of

Social and Economic Relations. In addition, Wesley Foundations, Methodist Youth Fellowships, and other student organizations were becoming increasingly involved with race relations issues and were supporting the student protest movement.[6]

The years that followed were filled with heightened activism and violent abuses against persons fighting for equality. The American consciousness concerning the horrors of racial injustice was raised when televised pictures of beatings and killings of black and white civil rights workers and innocent children were shown. In August 1963, more than two hundred thousand blacks and whites participated in the March on Washington, which was designed to bring national attention to the racial issues confronting America.

From 1964 to 1968, Congress passed major legislation to end legalized segregation and discrimination: the Civil Rights Act of 1964, the Voting Rights Act of 1965, and the Fair Housing Act of 1968. These gains did not occur devoid of tragedies. Shock and disillusionment reverberated throughout the nation as the country witnessed and experienced the assassinations of Medgar Evers (1963), President John F. Kennedy (1963), Malcom X (1965), Martin Luther King, Jr. (1968), and Robert Kennedy (1968). During these years, young black children became the first to integrate southern public schools in the midst of hostile taunts of racial slurs hurled by angry whites, while in some cities, armed soldiers were necessary to serve as their shield and protectors.

With assistance from thousands of northern and southern college students who flocked to southern cities to support the implementation of the Voting Rights Act and with bold courage and confidence in their God, blacks, who had been conditioned by the threat of death after years of intimidation by and fear of the Klu Klux Klan, began to register and exercise their hard earned right to vote—electing the first black officials to public offices across the South.

In August 1965, I graduated from Morgan State College
in Baltimore, where I was a political science major, debater,
and student activist. After graduation, I began work with
Congressman Charles McC. Mathias, Jr., of Maryland.
Gloster, Jr., an honor student, finance major, and debater at
Howard University, became president of the student government, and John David began middle school.

In the midst of these events, the Richmond Public
School system finally initiated its desegregation plan.
Several black students were selected to attend John Marshall High School, an all-white school. Leontine, who
many said was "preaching" history and economics in
the classroom, strongly believed that the selected students should not be alone as they faced this difficult, and
to some degree, treacherous challenge. Along with nine
other black teachers, she agreed to teach at John Marshall High School. However, her decision to leave Armstrong was a controversial one, and the principal of
Armstrong, who had always been a supportive administrator, was angry and disappointed with her for choosing to transfer to John Marshall.

This period of racial turbulence found many black
Methodists actively involved in the struggle for inclusiveness in society and constantly questioning their loy-
alty and commitment to their racially exclusive
denomination. They pushed harder for The Methodist
Church to be faithful to its Wesleyan principles and
Social Creed. Bishop James Thomas wrote that the Central Jurisdiction Study Committee ("Committee of Five")
stated in its report: "We believe that an inclusive
Methodist Church is a society of persons whose life and
practice are based on the great Christian affirmation of
unity and oneness of all believers in Christ." The report
further stated: "To recapitulate, the basic goal of our
endeavors, at least as the Committee of Five views it,
must be a Methodist Church completely free at all levels

of church life of distinctions based on race or color. That means that all forms of racial segregation and discrimination must be eliminated."[7]

From 1960 to 1964, increasing numbers of black Methodist leaders articulated the need for the denomination to eliminate the racially segregated Central Jurisdiction, and they organized to actively demonstrate their dissatisfaction with the divided structure at the 1964 General Conference. Major Jones writes that "the elimination of the Central Jurisdiction was one of the central concerns of the 1964 General Conference when it convened in Pittsburgh, Pennsylvania, in April, 1964. . . . There were pickets, there were calls for redress of many current social ills and glaring injustices, so rampant in American society in those times."[8]

At the 1964 General Conference, The Methodist Church decreed: "All local churches should be opened to all persons without regard to race, color, or national origin or economic condition" . . . adopted a detailed plan of action for the elimination of the Central Jurisdiction, created a temporary general aid fund to undergird the salaries and pensions of pastors in the Central Jurisdiction, and formed a Jurisdiction Advisory Council to work within each Jurisdiction on transfers and mergers.[9]

Following the General Conference, the seventh session of the Central Jurisdictional Conference was held at Bethune-Cookman College in Daytona Beach, Florida, in June 1964. The Central Jurisdiction Study Committee's report was adopted and boundaries of its annual conferences were realigned so that each conference fell within bounds of only one of the five respective regional jurisdictions.[10] Also during this session, James S. Thomas became the thirteenth bishop to be elected by the Central Jurisdiction. The Committee on Episcopacy assigned Bishop M. Lafayette Harris to the Atlantic Coast Area, Bishop Prince A. Taylor, Jr., to the Baltimore Area,

Bishop James S. Thomas to the Chicago Area, Bishop Charles F. Golden to the Nashville-Greensboro Area, and Bishop Noah W. Moore to the Southwestern Area.[11]

Soon after the meeting, the Delaware and Washington Annual Conferences transferred, or merged, into the Northeastern Jurisdiction with Bishop Prince Taylor ceasing to be a bishop of the Central Jurisdiction and becoming a bishop of the Northeastern Jurisdiction, New Jersey Area. The North Central Jurisdiction, at its meeting in Cleveland, on July 8-12, 1964, voted the official transfer of the Lexington Annual Conference from the Central Jurisdiction into the North Central Jurisdiction. Bishop James Thomas ceased to be bishop of the Chicago Area of the Lexington Conference and was assigned to the North Central Jurisdiction, Iowa Area.

During this time, David Kelly, who enjoyed fishing, became familiar with an area called Northern Neck, Virginia, and fell in love with Edwardsville, Virginia, a little fishing community in Northumberland County where the Chesapeake Bay flows into the Potomac River. It was in the Edwardsville area that he and Leontine decided to build their retirement home. David purchased several acres and sold two major lots to ministerial colleagues—one to Joseph B. Bethea, who was elected to the episcopacy in 1988, and one to John Carrington. On a two-acre lot located about a half mile from the beach, David built a house in the midst of the woods.

A small congregation of black Methodists, whose descendants had founded Galilee Methodist Episcopal Church in the late 1870s, was also located in Edwardsville. Its membership consisted of families who resided in the community and had sustained their church for almost one hundred years. The church had never had a full-time salaried pastor, but periodically students from Howard University's Divinity School served as supply pastors. The church was nestled back off the road and surrounded by pine and birch trees. The gray wooden building had a bell tower that leaned from years of witnessing the hopes, fears, sorrows, and joys of those who entered the sanctuary. Facing the pulpit and potbellied stoves, the men, many of whom fished the waters of Maryland and Virginia (and often had to go as far south as Louisiana to get enough fish to sell to make a decent living), always sat on the right; the women, who worked in the fisheries, the Levi plant, or commuted to another town for work, always sat on the left. Lacking a working piano, an elder would line out the hymns while others, picking up the tune, repeated the line and patted their feet to establish and maintain the rhythm.

In Richmond, David had successfully enabled Leigh Street Methodist Church to relocate from the downtown area by purchasing Mechanicsville Methodist Church (renamed Wesley Methodist Church) from white Methodists who were fleeing the neighborhood because blacks were buying homes in the area. This was during the period when annual conferences aligned under the Central Jurisdictional structure were beginning to merge with their white geographic counterparts. Black Methodist churches in Virginia had been part of the Washington Conference; in 1964, however, the Washington Conference transferred into the Northeastern Jurisdiction. Since white, Virginia Methodists were not ready for merger—and did not merge until 1968—black churches in Virginia were realigned under the Nashville-Carolina Episcopal Area, which included Tennessee-Kentucky, North Carolina and South Carolina.[12] David, however, had no interest in being appointed to a church in North or South Carolina and anticipated that black Methodist churches in Virginia would eventually merge into the Virginia Conference of the Southeastern Jurisdiction. Having completed his work with Wesley Methodist Episcopal Church, David retired to Northumberland County, maneuvering a part-time appointment to Galilee Methodist Church. Leontine remained in Richmond for another year so John David could complete junior high school, and on the weekends, they commuted to Edwardsville.

During that year of transition to Edwardsville, one of David's grandchildren, from a previous marriage, came to Richmond with David's eighteen-month-old great-granddaughter, Pamela Lynne, and arranged for Pam to live with David and Leontine. A few years after David's death, when Pam was five years old, Lenontine initiated action to formally adopt Pam; and she became Leontine's fourth child and second daughter.

CHAPTER SEVEN

Galilee

As Methodists around the world engaged in the politics of merger, the members of Galilee Church, with the daily pastoral leadership of David Kelly, began to envision the variety of ministries that were needed for the children, youth, and adults within their community and a new church facility that could accommodate those ministries. In the midst of their planning process, David was diagnosed with cancer and died in March of 1969.

A few weeks after David's death, the leaders of Galilee told the Reverend Joseph Carson, the district superintendent, that they wished for "Ms. Kelly" to serve as their interim pastor. Knowing she was a licensed lay speaker, Carson asked Leontine to "hold the church together" until the annual conference. In June 1969, Leontine was officially appointed to Galilee as a supply pastor.

Leontine had been teaching full time at Northumberland High School since the move to Edwardsville and continued to do so while she conducted Sunday morning worship services, kept the various church committees functioning, and provided leadership to the church trustees and administrative board members as they implemented the planning and fund development processes to build a new church.

Financial institutions in rural Virginia did not have a

history of supporting the black community; subsequently, Galilee ran into a brick wall in its efforts to obtain construction financing. The Reverend Carson, having assisted white Methodist churches in securing construction loans, was surprised when bank officers, a few of whom were influential Methodists, were not willing to assist Galilee. In a conversation with Leontine, she recalled that following an evening meeting with the district superintendent and several church leaders regarding their inability to obtain financial support, she had a dream:

> It was morning, and Leontine went downstairs and saw David Kelly in their living room, smoking his pipe. He smiled, assured her she was doing all the right things with Galilee, and instructed her to call Dr. Dennis Fletcher at the Methodist Board of Missions at 10 a.m. the next day to solicit his assistance with obtaining the funds for the building project. David told her to go to the file cabinet in his office in the house and open the file labeled "Galilee Building." In the file were the answers to three questions that she would need to answer when she talked with Dennis Fletcher.

When she awoke the next morning, Leontine went to the file cabinet in David's office. She found the file mentioned in the dream and discovered the three questions and their answers just as David had said. She woke John David for school and shared with him the vision and what had occurred.

When she arrived at the high school, she made arrangements with the principal to call the Board of Missions at ten o'clock that morning. Using the telephone in the principal's office, Leontine called Dr. Fletcher, who answered the phone himself. She introduced herself and shared the purpose of her call. Dr. Fletcher replied that he had just returned from California and, while there, had had dinner with her brother DeWitt, who was the pastor of Crenshaw United Methodist Church in Los Angeles. Leontine asked if David Kelly, prior to his death, had discussed Galilee's building project with Dr. Fletcher. Dr. Fletcher indicated that he had not had any conversation with David and then proceeded to ask the three questions that were in the file folder. Leontine provided the answers as recorded, and Dr. Fletcher made arrangements to visit Galilee. Shortly thereafter, Dr. Fletcher came to Edwardsville and met with Mr. Carson and the church leaders. Following his review, Fletcher told the district superintendent that, based upon his assessment of Galilee's financial plans and the assurance that Leontine would remain the pastor, he would recommend the directors of the Board of Missions approve a $25,000 direct grant and a $40,000 loan for Galilee to build its church. When Mr. Carson questioned whether this proposal would be approved, it is said that Dr. Fletcher assured Mr. Carson that he had worked for twenty-five years at the Board of Missions and that all of his recommendations had been approved.

Galilee received approval and funding support from the Board of Missions, as well as contributions from every church under Mr. Carson's leadership in the Rappahanock District. With excitement and great expectations for the future, they broke ground for the new church. The new facility would provide not only a lovely sanctuary but a well-equipped kitchen, classroom space, fellowship hall, and indoor plumbing—a first for many in that area. Many homes in the Edwardsville community did not have indoor plumbing until later when Shiloh Baptist Church in Reedsville, Virginia, and Galilee solicited support for a rural housing development project from the federal government.

As Leontine ministered to the people of Galilee, she was inspired by the growing number of women taking public stands in the political and denominational arenas. In turn, she inspired the young people of Galilee to envision a better future for themselves. As the first black teacher at Northumberland County High School, and now the pastoral leader of many of the students, Leontine was determined to have her students graduate from high school and experience opportunities historically not available to young people residing in the area. She believed, and encouraged them to believe, that they could "soar like eagles." She worked with the high school counselor and helped find scholarship funds for one of Galilee's young women, Martha Elmore, to go to college.

Martha was the first member of Galilee Church to accomplish what was inconceivable for many. One memorable day in January 1974, three generations of black women—Martha, her mother, her grandmother, and Leontine—ascended the steps of St. Paul's College in Lawrenceville, Virginia, to enroll Martha in school. With tears of joy and thanksgiving streaming down their faces, they burst forth in songs of praise to God as they marveled at God's goodness. Martha graduated from St. Paul's four years later with a degree in education and became the stimulus for other Galileans to vision a new life of possibilities and prepare themselves for a new and different future.

Word spread, and people began hearing of Leontine, this unique personality who had followed her husband into the ministry. She was engaging the Galilee members in a building campaign, exposing and involving them in the program ministries of the annual conference, and responding to the social issues within the county and surrounding communities—and she could preach! Her contributions did not go unnoticed by church officials in high places either. Bishop William Ragsdale Cannon, who served as the Episcopal leader of the Richmond Area, 1970–1972, stated in his autobiography, *A Magnificent Obsession*:

> The black minister in Virginia who had done by far the most outstanding work and whom I wanted to appoint a district superintendent in that conference unfortunately did not satisfy the technical requirements of the office, and by the law of the Church was forbidden from holding it. That person was a woman who had entered the ministry following the death of her husband, who had been a prominent preacher in the Virginia Conference, and who felt the call to take up where he left off. At this time she was only an approved supply pastor. She had not begun her seminary education.[1]

Though Leontine had been appointed to pastor Galilee, she strongly believed that one could not be ordained unless they themselves had experienced "The Call" from God. She initially felt she was just filling in at Galilee until the conference could find an ordained person to appoint. In addition to pastoring part-time, Leontine was still teaching full-time, was trying to adjust to life without David, and was handling the parenting responsibilities for three-year-old Pam and teenage son John David. In addition, Ila, now eighty-six years old, had decided that Teenie needed Ila "to take care of her," after David's death, so Ila left Cincinnati and moved to Edwardsville.

In the midst of all these responsibilities, God did call Leontine:

It was the summer of 1969, and having seen that Dr. Ted Landis, a clergyman who I respected, was to teach a course on the inner life at the Virginia Conference United Methodist Women's School of Mission to be held in Lynchburg, I registered Mama and myself to attend. Three weeks before school was to begin, I received a call from the chair indicating that Dr. Landis's three classes on the inner life were booked, and they needed to structure another class and would I teach it. I said, "I can't teach the inner life to anybody! I need to take it! My own inner life is fragmented and I have many unanswered questions in the midst of my own lament and I'm still asking the Lord many questions." The caller responded, "Well, pray on it, and we will get you certified and send the materials for you to use in preparation for the class."

I prayed all night and tried to get off the hook, but couldn't. When I received the materials from the Mission Center of the General Board of Global Ministries, it included a special resource by Dr. Harvey Potthoff, professor of Christian Theology at Iliff School of Theology: *The Inner Life: A Study Book*. I felt good working with the subject and developing the course.

On the first day of the class, an elderly black minister from Eastern Shore, Virginia, named the Reverend Hori Spencer, who was a friend of my father and brother DeWitt, came into my classroom. Having heard that he was very ill, I inquired as to why he was there. He replied, "I heard you were teaching a course on the inner life, and I needed to be here."

By the fourth day of teaching, it was very clear to me that the class was experiencing the powerful presence of the Holy Spirit. I instructed each of them to return to their room and observe the Benedictine silence until after supper, reflecting upon why the class was being blessed with the presence of the Holy Spirit and what it meant for each of them. When everyone had left the class, as I was exiting, the Reverend Spencer, the last to leave, said to me, "Teenie, you might as well do it now."

I knew what he meant: that I needed to accept my calling to the ordained ministry. Then I returned to my room, and during prayer, I felt assured of what I needed to do: that I would have to give up teaching. I knew that I had to trust that the mortgage note on the home David and I had built would be taken care of, that I had to be strong enough to help my mother understand that she couldn't take care of me, that I had to take care of myself! For the first time since David's death, I felt a strength I had not experienced before. I knew that God had called me to the ordained ministry.[2]

Two weeks later, Leontine attended Mr. Spencer's funeral and learned from his wife that after he left Leontine's class, he told his wife he was ready to return home, that he had accomplished what the Lord had sent him there to do.

Leontine began her theological training by enrolling in the License School for Local Pastors in 1970 and completed three years of the Ministerial Course of Study Program of The United Methodist Church through correspondence courses and the Wesley Course of Study School at Wesley Theological Seminary. According to Leontine, one of her courses of study teachers, Dr. Earl Hubert Furgesen, encouraged her to enter the Master's in Divinity program; however, with her family and church responsibilities, she did not see how she could enroll at Wesley full time. The day she accepted her call, she remembers saying: "Lord, I don't want to bargain with you, but I would love to be a trained minister. But with John David enrolling in college, there is no money for me to attend seminary." A year later, another interesting experience occurred.

In the early 1970s, Virginia's Northumberland County still had limited and segregated medical facilities. African American residents requiring surgery or extensive medical care had to go to Richmond, a three hour drive, for hospitalization. Galileans were no exception, and many of Leontine's members were often hospitalized at the historically black hospital, Richmond Memorial. Returning to Edwardsville after a trip to Richmond to visit sick members and the annual conference office, Leontine pulled into the parking lot of the Presbyterian-affiliated Union Theological Seminary. After asking herself what she was doing at the seminary, she went to the registrar's office. The registrar was away, but one of the school's professor's was present, and she said to him: "I hardly know what I'm doing here, and on paper it makes no sense for me to think seriously about going to seminary full time—with a mortgage note, family responsibilities, and pastoring a church—but in prayer it does. Do you have any Presbyterian money with Methodist written on it?" He replied, "Yes, we do! We have a fund that only Methodist students can use." When Leontine left the campus, she had received a $2,500 scholarship, a furnished campus apartment, and had arranged to take the required Greek and Hebrew courses before enrolling in the degree program full-time.

When Gloster, Jr., and I were home visiting, Mama called a family meeting and shared her plans to enroll at Union Theological Seminary. I was serving as program director of the Ann Arbor Community Center, having received the Master of Social Work degree from the University of Michigan. Gloster, Jr., had completed his two years of military service with the Army, obtained a Master of Business Administration from the University of Pittsburgh, and begun his marketing career at Proctor and Gamble in Cincinnati. John David was enrolled at Virginia State College in Petersburg, Virginia.

The plan was to attend seminary full-time; Pam and Nana would go to Richmond with her, and she would commute back to Edwardsville on weekends to continue pastoring Galilee. She talked about her calling and how God was using her in this new way. Gloster, Jr., and I, still novices in our own spiritual growth and understanding, expressed concern about giving up her teaching position and the financial realities of paying the mortgage note, receiving a "minimum" salary, paying tuition and fees for John David's college expenses—as well as for herself—and living expenses for her, Nana, and Pam. Many people would have asked similar questions, for it certainly did not make economic sense. In fact, it appeared illogical for a middle-aged, African American woman who was the single parent of a five year old and caretaker of an aging mother to pursue another academic degree at age fifty. But her answer was filled with trust and conviction: "I don't know how it will be done, but I know that God will take care of it, that God will work it out!" God did work it out, beyond anybody's expectations!

On June 21, 1972, under the episcopal leadership of Bishop William R. Cannon at the Virginia annual conference, Leontine was ordained a deacon. She received her Master of Divinity degree from Union Theological Seminary in 1976 and was ordained an elder by Bishops Kenneth Goodson and E. L. Tullis on June 14, 1977.

During her six year pastorate at Galilee, she led the congregation in building a new edifice, paying off the construction loan, and building a four-bedroom ranch style parsonage. All of this was accomplished while she struggled through Greek and Hebrew, balanced seminary course work, nurtured and affirmed her children as they faced their own life battles, formally adopted Pam, and listened to criticizing comments that were often mixed with admiration and praise from her strong, tenacious, and domineering mother.

CHAPTER EIGHT

Barriers Broken

By the mid-1970s African Americans began to believe they were becoming "first-class citizens." The Vietnam War ended, and Richard Nixon resigned the presidency because of Watergate. The Voting Rights Act was empowering black people and allowing them to voice their opinions at the ballot box, and the Congressional Black Caucus was increasing in membership and legislative influence. During Jimmy Carter's presidency, Patricia Roberts Harris became the first woman to be appointed to the Cabinet as secretary of housing and urban development. Civil rights leader Andrew Young was appointed ambassador to the United Nations, and Randall Robinson founded TransAfrica, whose mission was to influence U.S. policies toward Africa and the Caribbean.

Gloster, Sr.'s career with the NAACP had reached its peak and was beginning to wane. His involvement in local and general church activities was providing a different type of stimulus for his creative talents and organizational capabilities. His fund-raising gifts were put to use for special projects at St. Paul Church, such as the organ campaign and roof replacement. His support and commitment to historically black Methodist colleges led to the establishment of and his service as the first chairperson of the Black College Fund Commission for the

New York Conference. In 1977, Gloster, Sr., was awarded honorary degrees by Methodist–affiliated Bethune-Cookman College in Daytona Beach and Rust College in Holly Springs, Mississippi, for his civil rights leadership and his efforts in securing the financial stability of Methodist black colleges with the establishment of The Black College Fund as an apportioned fund within the denomination. His knowledge and musical gifts were utilized through his work as a member of the Board of Discipleship's Commission on Worship, while his skills as a political strategist helped to elect the African American bishops of the Northeastern Jurisdiction: Roy C. Nichols (1968), Edward G. Carroll (1972), F. Herbert Skeete (1980), Felton E. May (1984), and Forrest C. Stith (1984).

An active participant in the denomination's various merger-related processes resulting from the 1968 Uniting Conference, Gloster, Sr., was elected lay delegate to the General Conferences held in Atlanta (1972) and Portland, Oregon (1976). At the 1972 General Conference, Bishop F. Gerald Ensley delivered the Episcopal Address, citing the denomination's efforts within the past four years to ensure a smooth process for the merger of the Evangelical United Brethren Church and the Central Jurisdiction. He said:

> The United Methodist Church has grown steadily together. The Articles of Union of the Evangelical United Brethren Church and The Methodist Church permitted three quadrenniums—until 1980—for the assimilation of the annual conferences. Now in 1972—in one-third of the time allowed—all the former conferences have been joined. . . . All of us have profited by the marriage of the two denominations. No one has really lost by the union and much has been gained. . . .
>
> There has been a corresponding drawing together of black and white Methodists. Granted the pressure of events, there has been also the constraint of the

Christian ideal, one of the evidences of the Spirit's working. The miracle of union is taking place, defying the prophets of pessimism. The Central Jurisdiction has been dissolved. . . . The black members of clergy and laity have shown their capacity and willingness at every level to contribute to the Church. We have had new visions of how good and pleasant it is for men and women of differing races to dwell together.[1]

From 1968 through 1976, Gloster served as one of the initial members of the General Commission on Religion and Race, which was established at the 1968 General Conference. Bishop Kenneth Goodson served as chairman of the commission, and Reverend Woodie W. White, a member of the Detroit Conference, became the first Executive Secretary of the Commission. The Reverend Woodie White was elected to the episcopacy in 1984.

The General Commission on Religion and Race was established to foster a more inclusive community among the church's more than five hundred thousand ethnic minority persons and to ensure their participation at every level of the denomination's organizational life. The other African American members serving on the Commission were Bishop Charles P. Golden, John L. Bryan, Luther B. Felder, Sr., Dennis A. Fletcher, Warren M. Jenkins, Major J. Jones, Joseph E. Lowery, George E. Rice, Emmett Streeter, and Cecil Williams.[2] Hector Navas (Hispanic) also served with Gloster in the New York Conference and was elected secretary of the Commission.

During the first two quadrennia, the Commission concentrated its efforts on raising the consciousness of individuals and sensitizing the whole church to its racist attitudes and behavior patterns. They worked with annual conferences involved in merger, and they assessed the employment practices of the Church's boards and agencies. Recognizing the importance of increasing the Church's awareness of its purpose, the

Commission was determined that its meetings would be held in the geographic areas in the United States and Commonwealth of Puerto Rico where ethnic and racial minorities were concentrated. Scheduling commission meetings in the South where the civil rights of African Americans was still denied or under litigation in many towns and cities was a risky but intentional strategy used by commission members to challenge the segregation policies within the deep South.

Gloster, Sr., and Bishop Kenneth G. Goodson often traveled together in Mississippi and other southern states for these meetings. This was a major risk for them because segregationist policies and racist attitudes towards blacks were still quite prevalent and persons' lives were still often in jeopardy in many areas of the country despite the passage of civil rights laws.

In the years following the 1976 General Conference, Gloster served as a delegate to the 1976 World Methodist Assemby in Dublin, Ireland, chaired the New York Conference's Commission on Church and Society, and upon retirement from the NAACP in 1978, was appointed by Bishop W. Ralph Ward to serve as interim pastor of Westchester United Methodist Church in the Bronx.

Westchester United Methodist Church was located in a transitional racial-ethnic community. The church's membership, which was predominantly white, had declined significantly, resulting in only a few members attending Sunday services and serving in church leadership roles. With Rebecca's support and assistance, Gloster revitalized the music ministry by organizing a new sanctuary choir and establishing a children's choir and a youth gospel choir. As old members returned and new persons affiliated with Westchester, a unit of the United Methodist Women was reestablished, and the United Methodist Men, Council on Ministries, and Methodist Youth Fellowship became functional once again. Gloster continued his longtime support of young people by encouraging and assisting them in obtaining college educations and arranging for them to attend United Methodist schools.

Ironically, for one whose life's pathways had often placed him on the cutting edge, Gloster was now considered somewhat conservative by the "Young Turks." The Young Turks were a group of younger black ministerial colleagues in the New York Conference. Bishop F. Herbert Skeete, one of Gloster's protégés, recalled how Gloster and others might disagree on the strategy, but they always tried to find a way to support one another's position or issue.

Many throughout the church knew that although Gloster might publicly express chauvinistic attitudes toward women in ministry, he encouraged and defended many young women as they pursued their call. One of his former church members and daughters in the ministry, the Reverend Shirley Canty, was ordained in the New York Conference and became chaplain at Bennett College. Another, Dr. Linda Thomas Hopkins, was also ordained in the New York Conference and serves as professor of anthropology and religion at Lutheran Theological Seminary.

Reappointed to Westchester United Methodist Church by Bishop Roy Nichols, Gloster served until 1983, when Dr. Benjamin Hooks, executive director of the NAACP, appointed him to a one-year term as the NAACP's deputy executive director.

Throughout his life, Gloster stayed close to his children. From childhood to adulthood, GBC monitored and encouraged our educational development. When Gloster, Jr., and I were in college, he had a habit of initiating family debates on current events as a way of challenging our intellectual and analytical skills. He taught the values of work and the importance of using one's talents to improve opportunities for the less fortunate. Through letters and weekly telephone calls to us, he expressed his concern and support, and he did not hesitate to question one's decision making if he thought it irresponsible or insensible. As he grew older, he found it easier to more openly express his love and pride in his children's accomplishments and share in their achievements.

In his senior years he continued to be an active participant in church and national affairs. He served on the board of directors for the National Caucus for the Black Aged, was national parliamentarian for the National Association of Negro Musicians, was president of the United Methodist New York City Society, and was elected a delegate by the New York Conference to the 1984 and 1988 General Conferences. From 1984 to 1992, he served as director of the General Board of Discipleship and chaired the Institutional Racism Committee (1984–1988). He greatly enjoyed his work with the Book of Worship Committee, which produced a new *Book of Worship* to accompany the new 1989 *United Methodist Hymnal*. Gloster, Sr., ended his active church career playing the organ at St. Paul United Methodist Church, which he did until the age of eighty-two.

On July 3, 1997, Gloster Bryant Current, Sr., transitioned from this life and joined the saints. On July 9, 1997, Bishop F. Herbert Skeete (retired), Bishop Ernest Lyght (episcopal leader of the New York Annual Conference), lay and clergy members of the New York Annual Conference, officials of the NAACP, officers of the National Association of Negro Musicians, pastors and members of St. Paul United Methodist Church, and many friends and colleagues joined with his family in the celebration of his life of service to God, the Methodist Church, and the people.

CHAPTER NINE

Make Plain the Vision[1]

The 1970s spawned a rekindling of the woman's movement in America, regaining a national visibility that was similar to its exposure during the early 1900s when the campaign for woman's suffrage resulted in the passage of the Nineteenth Amendment to the Constitution, giving women full voting rights.

Though one of the few African American ordained clerywomen in the denomination, Leontine, as well as her commitment to forging ahead in her ministry, was reinforced by the growing swell of women across the country and the international demand for a more gender inclusive society. Increasing numbers of African American women were "challenging the barriers of racism and sexism that burdened minority women within their racial communities and in the larger society."[2] In 1972, the General Assembly of the United Nations, "against a background of rising demands for equal rights and responsibilities among women the world over," proclaimed 1975 as "International Women's Year," sponsored the World Conference of the International Women's Year in Mexico City, and proclaimed the United Nations Decade for Women, 1975-1985. Their historic proclamation outlined the following aims:

> To promote equality between men and women; to ensure the full integration of women in the total

development effort, especially by emphasizing women's responsibility and important role in economic, social, and cultural development at the national, regional, and international level, particularly during the Second United Nations Development Decade; and to recognize the importance of women's increasing contribution to the development of friendly relations and cooperation among States, and to the strengthening of world peace.[3]

United Methodist women were being led by such strong, visionary leaders as Thelma Stevens (1902–1990), executive secretary of the Department of Christian Social Relations and Local Church Activities; Theressa Hoover, the first African American woman to serve as associate general secretary of the Women's Division and later deputy general secretary of the Board of Global Ministries; Mai Grey, president of the Women's Division (1976-1980); Rose Catchings, functional secretary for the Ministry of Women, World Division, Board of Global Ministries (1967-1988); Dr. Trudie Preciphs Reed (1976–1985), executive secretariat of the General Commission on the Status and Role of Women; the Reverend Nancy Grissom Self (1976-1994); and Kiyoko Kasai Fujiu (1977–1991). They, along with thousands of other Methodist women, challenged, sensitized, and educated the Church and its leaders to be more responsive to the social issues of the world and the needs of women and children, and they called for more inclusiveness of women in leadership and decision-making roles within the denomination.

Responding to petitions from the Women's Division, the 1968 Uniting Conference authorized a study commission to conduct research on the participation of women in the program and policy-making areas of The United Methodist Church. The commission was charged with the responsibility of fostering an awareness of problems and issues related to the status and role of women—with special reference to full participation in the total life of the Church at least commensurate with their total membership in The United Methodist Church.[4] In addition to these women's organizations, other minority caucuses such as the National Black Methodists for Church Renewal—led by Dr. Cain Felder, executive director, and the Reverend Gilbert Caldwell, chair—voiced concerns regarding inclusiveness and parity for Methodist persons of color. At the 1972 General Conference in Atlanta, a new Commission on the Status and Role of Women was established for a larger minority of Methodists.

As women's issues were beginning to receive national visibility, several experiences enhanced Leontine's ministerial and spiritual growth while she was in seminary. She began broadening her involvement within the denomination. She served on the Health and Welfare Division of the Board of Global Ministries, was a member of the General Council on Ministries for two quadrennia, and became more vocal about the role of black Methodists in the newly formed United Methodist Church. Recalling one of her experiences she said:

> We had come from all over the country to the Retreat Center at Marysville, Kentucky in response to a call from the General Council on Ministries to help interpret and implement the General Conference's approved quadrennial emphasis: "Strengthening the Ethnic Minority Local Church." I had been asked to preach. Primarily, the occasion was a great reunion, especially for those of us accustomed to the closeness experienced in the Central Jurisdiction. Our deliberations made clear, we sought to define what it meant to be loyal to a major Caucasian

denomination that had historically paid minimal attention to its racial ethnic members, who had been loyal to the denomination despite racism and little interest in their presence. I recall being particularly inspired by members of the group who had come and who committed themselves to work for an inclusive church at every level. I was a seminarian pastoring a rural black church in Virginia. I knew the struggle of the people to remain connectional. I do not recall my text, I only remember the empowerment of the Holy Spirit that encompassed all present. The witness was sure! We were inspired to help our Church, The United Methodist Church, live up to its own pronouncements.[5]

As Leontine was about to complete her theological training, an invitation to preach the revival at Arlington United Methodist Church in Arlington, Virginia, resulted in another inspiring and powerful spiritual experience. When she returned home from Arlington, the host pastor called to notify her that the chief of the United States Chaplaincy had been at the revival every night she preached. He advised her not to be surprised if she received a call inviting her to preach to the Armed Forces. A few weeks later, she received an official invitation to go to the American Army bases of the European Command for the United States Chaplaincy and serve as the speaker for the Protestant Women of the Chapel Conference in Berchtesgaden, Germany. It was her last semester, and the three week tour coincided with the seminary's three week spring quarter. When she shared the news with Dean Neely McCarter at Union Theological Seminary, he concurred that this unusual opportunity was a valuable experience for any seminary student and merited being substituted for the three week course she was to take.

Upon graduation, Bishop Kenneth Goodson, episcopal leader of the Virginia annual conference, recognizing her gifts and ability to work with people, appointed Leontine associate program council director for the Virginia Annual Conference Council on Ministries. Though the appointment was a promotion and provided a salary increase, leaving Galilee was not easy. The people had "loved" her into the ministry and had trusted her leadership; together they had had life changing experiences that had accomplished much!

Eighteen months later, as Pam enrolled in elementary school and Nana became more feeble, Leontine found it necessary to share with the bishop the negative effect the heavy meeting and travel schedule that was related to her assignments as program council director was having on her role as mother and caretaker. After this conversation, Bishop Goodson appointed Leontine to Asbury United Methodist Church on Church Hill in Richmond, Virginia. She also served as the director of Church Hill Urban Ministry (CHUM), an outreach program of the Church involving the Richmond District and the Virginia Conference. The program, utilizing neighborhood teenagers, provided after-school tutorial assistance and summer educational development for elementary and middle school children, assisted neighborhood residents with their human service needs, and engaged in community organization and community development activities.

Under her leadership, CHUM became a model community service project, and her involvement with the Church Hill community led to her actively serving as a member of the Richmond Public School Board for four years. During the six years that Leontine pastored Asbury, the church's membership increased. In addition, the church had a vital youth gospel choir, and its services to the community were recognized and appreciated by neighborhood residents and community leaders.

In January 1979, several black clergywomen joined more than 650 persons gathered in Dallas for the second National Consultation for United Methodist Clergy-women. Leontine attended and, though impressed with the number of black participation on the leadership level, expressed concern that the Consultation lacked a workshop on urban ministry, which was vital to many black churches located in the inner cities across the nation.

By the 1980s women across denominational lines were increasingly responding to their call to ministry, taking their place in the pulpit, and being appointed to key administrative leadership roles within the church. Based on interviews with twelve clergy sisters who became bishops, district superintendents and staff members of general agencies of the church during the last decade of the twentieth century, the Reverend Barbara B. Troxell wrote:

> In the last third of the twentieth century, certain United Methodist clergywomen said yes to the call of the church to become district superintendents and bishops. . . . After serving several rural churches, including a seven point charge, the Reverend Margaret Hendrichsen was appointed superintendent of the Bangor (now Northern) District of the Maine Annual Conference, the first woman superintendent in The Methodist Church within the continental United States. Then, in 1980, after serving as superintendent of the Grand Traverse District of the West Michigan Annual Conference, Marjorie Swank Matthews was elected bishop, the first woman in any large Christian denomination to serve.[6]

In 1981, Lynn Norment wrote, "In marbled sanctuaries on city streets and in tiny churches on dusty country roads, a different kind of voice is heard preaching the gospel these days—the voice of an increasing number of female pastors. Despite opposition from some hard-line male clergymen who still have difficulty accepting women in the pulpit, some Black women are not deterred from leading their own congregations."[7]

Leontine and nine other clergywomen, including her United Methodist clergy sister, the Reverend Tallulah F. Williams, a district superintendent in the Northern Illinois Conference, were featured in the article. Like many clergywomen, Leontine faced opposition from some male clergy, regardless of their race, because they had difficulty accepting women in the pulpit. Leontine was not deterred, and she would often refer to 1 Timothy 2:11-12 and proudly challenge audiences by saying, "I know what Paul said, but Paul didn't call me—God did!"

The demand for her to speak to various religious, civic, and community organizations around the country began to increase. She delivered the Earl Lectures at the Pacific School of Religion in 1980 and, in recognition of her skill in preaching and teaching, was asked to deliver the 1982 Georgia Harkness Lectureship at Garrett Evangelical Seminary in Evanston, Illinois. Many were inspired by Leontine's preaching style, which was rooted in the black tradition. As she moved across the pulpit or descended into the auditorium engaging the audience, her prophetic sermons highlighted the social justice issues within the community, raised consciousness, and called persons to accountability. Many persons, in and out of the Church, began to recognize and respond to the proclaiming of the gospel through this new and anointed voice that called them to remember and live their covenant relationship with God.

With support from the Virginia Conference Commission on the Status and Role of Women, which was chaired by Dr. Diedra Kriewald, Leontine was the first clerywoman elected delegate by the Virginia Conference to the 1980 General Conference, which met in Indianapolis. At that General Conference, Leontine chaired the Committee on Independent Commissions and, at one of the worship services held for conference attendees, served as liturgist for the Reverend Joe A. Harding, a noted evangelist and senior pastor at Central United Protestant Church in Richland, Washington.

In July 1980, Leontine served as a delegate to the Southeastern Jurisdictional Conference, which was held at Lake Junaluska Assembly in North Carolina. Encouraged by many lay and clergywomen who felt the time had come for a woman to be elected to the episcopacy, Leontine was asked to consider the position seriously. Recognizing the risk of ridicule, she allowed her name to be placed in nomination. Veteran power brokers for episcopal elections were shocked; they felt her nomination audacious, as well as ridiculous, and she was not elected.

Then unprecedented events began to occur. In June 1983, Leontine was appointed assistant general secretary for the section on evangelism, The United Methodist Board of Discipleship and relocated to Nashville. This was the first appointment of an African American clergywoman to this position. Her job included coordinating the work of the national evangelism staff as they conducted training workshops; providing information and technical assistance to annual conferences, districts, and local churches in their efforts to recruit and nurture congregations and individuals as disciples of Jesus Christ; and preaching God's word throughout The United Methodist Church.

The new position was timely because, for the first time in her life, Leontine had an empty nest and was home alone. Fifteen years had passed since David's death, and she had come into her own. Nana, ninety-eight years old and requiring professional nursing care, moved from Asbury's parsonage to the Methodist Home in Richmond. John David had graduated from Emory-Riddle Aeronautics University and was living in Jos, Nigeria as the field treasurer for the United Methodist General Board of Global Ministries with his first wife, Minerva, and daughter, Faith. Pam, graduated with honors from high school, was to enroll that fall at Spelman College in Atlanta.

Leontine's year at the Board of Discipleship was filled with speaking engagements and travel throughout the country. The Reverend Kathy Nickerson Sage, staff in the Division of Ordained Ministry of the General Board of Higher Education and Ministry, asked her to cochair, with the Reverend Sharon Brown Christopher, the National Clergywomen's Consultation held in Glorietta, New Mexico. The Reverend Liz Lopez Spence captured the purpose of the consultation in her sermon at Glorietta: "We come to new visions in our lives as they are made plain by the visions of others. That is the journey of my own life. As I hear my sisters proclaim their journeys, my journey becomes easier to proclaim."[8] Reflecting on that historic gathering of women, Leontine recalled:

> Over one thousand clergywomen attended. The determination to include clergywomen at both the appointive and elective levels of the Church without discrimination because of sex was a goal. The election of women as bishops appeared to be a reality, for in 1980 it had happened! Marjorie Matthews was elected the first female bishop of any major denomination. All of us who experienced Glorietta knew that Convocation to be the source of inspiration for believing in a new day for the Church of Jesus Christ.[9]

At Glorietta, Leontine was endorsed for the episcopacy by a resolution of over 750 clergywomen. Their strategy was to place her name in nomination in four of the five jurisdictions that would meet simultaneously in July 1984. A committee of clergywomen, coordinated by her friend, Dr. Diedra Kriewald (Virginia Annual Conference), was formed to promote her candidacy. Helen Neinast served as corresponding secretary, and Karen Collier, Judith Weidman, Barbara Troxell, Nan Grissom Self, Susan Henry Crowe, Karla Kincannon, and many others across the country were instrumental in her candidacy.

It was understood that it would be difficult to elect a woman in the Southeastern Jurisdiction—and practically impossible to elect an African American woman—so letters were sent to all the women delegates in the Southeastern Jurisdiction Conference. During the annual meeting of the Southeastern Jurisdiction's Black Methodists for Church Renewal, Leontine solicited the support of black church leaders. Many of these leaders were ambivalent toward her candidacy because they feared that her being a black woman would negatively affect the candidacy of the black men aspiring for the episcopacy and reduce their chances, but some did affirm her as the women's candidate.

Leontine adopted the Convocation's theme, "Make Plain the Vision," and Habakkuk's words:

> Then the Lord answered me and said:
> Write the vision;
> make it plain on tablets,
> so that a runner may read it.
> For there is still a vision for the appointed time."
> (Hab. 2:2-3*a*)

Leontine described her call to the episcopacy as "a vision for the appointed time."

As prophesied, the vision was being made plain. The word spread that Leontine was one of several clergy-women who, after Glorietta, had agreed to seek election to the episcopacy, and it appeared that every time there would be a political tactic to hamper her visibility, another opportunity would emerge. In the spring of 1984, Leontine was invited to become the first woman to preach on the National Radio Pulpit of the National Council of Churches, the oldest continuous network radio program in the country.

Virginia conference politics prohibited her from receiving enough votes to be a delegate to the 1984 General Conference in Baltimore, which was a major disappointment for her; however, her responsibilities at the Board of Discipleship enabled her to attend. Weeks prior to jurisdictional conference, while visiting her mother, Nana announced, "Teenie, you are going to be a bishop!" On June 16 Nana passed away—one month before her 102nd birthday.

The Psalmist said, "weeping may endure for a night, but joy *cometh* in the morning" (Ps. 30:5b KJV). On June 20, the Turpeau family celebrated the home going of its matriarch, Ila Marshall Turpeau, widow of the Reverend David Dewitt Turpeau, Sr., at Mount Zion United Methodist Church in Cincinnati. Less than four weeks later, Leontine went to Lake Junaluska to the Southeastern Jurisdiction quadrennial meeting hoping she might be elected to the episcopacy.

Leontine and her supporters talked to jurisdictional delegates in hopes of obtaining the required votes to be elected, but they had little success. On Tuesday evening, she received a call from her supporters in the Western Jurisdiction advising her to come to Boise, Idaho, immediately. They believed if the delegates had an opportunity to meet Leontine personally, she could obtain the support of the 60 percent required to be elected. The next day, after praying about the situation, she and Diedra Kriewald left Lake Junaluska and flew to Boise.

It was 2:00 A.M. Thursday, July 18, when Leontine arrived in Salt Lake City. A few minutes before catching the connecting flight to Boise, she remembered that I had arranged to be with her at Lake Junaluska, win or lose. She called to say that she was on her way to the Western Jurisdictional meeting in Boise. Still partially asleep, I assured her that I would meet her there. When I awoke and tried to make reservations for Boise, I discovered it was not an easy or inexpensive process. Fortunately, Gloster, Jr., who was attending a training conference in the Washington, D.C., area was staying at my home and was able to finance the trip. Thank God for brothers! By 9:30 A.M. Thursday morning, July 19, I was on a flight to Boise, but at one point, realizing that I was asleep when mother had called, I questioned whether she had said Idaho or Iowa.

When the plane landed, shades of orange intermingled with the blue clear Idaho sky as the sun set upon the horizon. As I stepped onto the tarmac, I realized that I did not know where the jurisdictional meeting was being held. Since most major cities have a First United Methodist Church, I called the church and was assured that the meeting was being held there. As the cab circled the full square block where the stately "Cathedral of the Rockies" stood, my heart pounded with excitement and anxiety as the area appeared deserted, and the doors were locked. Perhaps it was the wrong place!

Somewhat confused, I finally found the right door and asked a gentleman if he knew where I might find the Reverend Leontine Kelly. Another man came forward saying that the Reverend Kelly had gone to dinner on the campus of Boise State University. When I explained why I was there the man's eyes lit up. He excitedly shared that he was a minister, and though he had heard stories about the Holy Spirit, he had never actually felt its presence. He smiled as he repeated how Leontine Kelly had responded to the delegates' questions about her calling to the episcopacy, proclaiming that if "God didn't want her to be elected, she didn't want to be a bishop!" He then admitted that it was during those moments that, for the first time in his life, while listening to her, it happened. He felt the Holy Spirit! "Did she get elected?" I asked. He clapped his hands and said, "Yes! Praises be to God!"

The election itself proved to be what many would call miraculous. It was, without question, historic! Of the nineteen bishops elected during that week of jurisdictional conferences, the Western Jurisdiction produced the first Japanese American bishop, the Reverend Roy Sano, professor at Pacific School of Religion in Berkeley, California; the first Hispanic bishop, the Reverend Elias Galvan of Pasadena, California, director of the Council on Ministries for the Pacific and Southwest Conference; and the first African American woman bishop, the Reverend Leontine Turpeau Current Kelly.

Friday, July 20, 1984, was a glorious and historic day. The sun was shining brightly, and many believed God and the clouds of witnesses were smiling and rejoicing. First United Methodist Church of Boise, Idaho, was filled to capacity. The halls and auditorium were buzzing with excitement. Hawaiian leis of lavender and pink orchids were place around the necks of the special guests and family members of the bishops to be consecrated. I had on a purple Nigerian dress, which, for me, was symbolic of the presence of the ancestors, and the lavender orchids blended perfectly with it. The grand pipe organ swelled with the sounds of E. Gigout's "Grand Chorus Dialogue," and the conference choir sang Hopson's "Festival Psalm" as the choral introit. Some experienced goose bumps while others felt their eyes fill with tears as they reflected upon God's amazing grace, the events of the week, and this unique and special occasion.

Then the trumpets, trombones, and French horns proclaimed the arrival of the appointed time, and the organist played the hymn of the clergy, "God of Love and God of Power" as the marshall and selected persons entered the sanctuary, carrying the cross, episcopal banner, and shepherd's crook. The acolytes were followed by a procession of the College of Bishops of the Western Jurisdiction: Wilbur Choy, Calvin McConnell, Jack Tuell, Melvin Talbert, and Marvin Stuart. Bishop W. Kenneth Goodson, who had ordained Leontine an elder, represented the Council of Bishops; Bishop Herman L. Anderson represented the African Methodist Episcopal Zion Church; and Bishop Nathaniel Lindsey, who had befriended David and Leontine when they pastored in Knoxville, represented The Christian Methodist Episcopal Church.

During the Act of Consecration, the Reverend Leontine Turpeau Current Kelly knelt before the altar as the bishops and assisting elders, Barbara Troxell and Diedra Kriewald, laid their hands upon her head. Leontine's journey to this place and high position in the church was divinely guided. Contrary to what some believe, it was not because of sophisticated political strategies, but it was a part of God's masterful plan to be revealed in its own time. I was asked by Mother to represent the family, and I placed my hand along with the others upon her head. In that special moment I sensed that I was the conduit through which the blessings of the ancestors from both sides of the family were passed on to Mother.

As persons recounted the jurisdictional deliberations at the Cathedral of the Rockies, many African American Methodists understood that Leontine's historic rise to the episcopacy is rooted in the life ministries and service of those persons who influenced her life's journey and her subsequent willingness to respond to God's call to ministry. Leontine's consecration represented the culmination of efforts made by a people who believed that, by faith and God's redeeming grace, all things are possible. It represented a coming together of the sacrifices and contributions to society that were made by her forebears through the institutionalized church, specifically the Methodist Church. It proved to be another example of God choosing ordinary people as God's prophets and servants. It proved that if they are obedient and adhere to God's will, extraordinary things can happen in their lives.

It had not been an easy journey. Like most peoples' journeys on the pathway of life, there were twists and turns, barriers and obstacles, love lost and found, joys and sorrows, and celebrations of accomplishments in spite of the odds, that had brought her to this place in time. The royal threads that wove the tapestry of holy boldness that she wore so well began long before she was born. It was fashioned by blacks and whites, men and women, people who believed in a God who would open doors in the mist of what seemed impossible. A God who enabled freed slaves, educated by the Church to use their gifts and talents, to improve the quality of life for their people. A God who allowed the slave masters to use the Christian gospel to pacify the slaves; but the slaves, who heard the liberating good news of the gospel of Jesus Christ, became empowered and eventually free from the oppressor.

Those close to Leontine believed that her election was providential. They remembered the family story and the words spoken by Bishop Matthew W. Clair, Sr., as he christened this girl child of Ila and David, on June 6, 1920: "Oh, how I wish you were a boy so that I could place my mantle upon you." Now, it was done! God's mantle was placed upon her, and God continued to use her in incredible and extraordinary ways.

CHAPTER TEN

Amazing Grace

Leontine's election was historic for many reasons. At the age of sixty-four, she was the first African American woman to be elected bishop of any mainline Protestant denomination in the world, and she remained the only one until Barbara C. Harris was elected a suffragan bishop by the Episcopal Church in 1989. Leontine was the second woman to be chosen as a bishop in The United Methodist Church. Her election by a jurisdiction that she was not a member of was also historic; for though Methodist history indicates that two or three persons have been elected from outside of their own jurisdiction, it remains a rare occurrence.[1]

The Western Jurisdictional Episcopal Committee assigned Leontine as the bishop of the San Francisco Area supervising the California-Nevada Conference—an ethnically diverse conference of Asian, African American, Hispanic, Native American, and Caucasian Methodists. The conference encompassed more than 100,000 members and 400 pastors in 386 churches in Northern California and Nevada. Her cabinet included: the Reverend Warner H. Brown, the Reverend Arturo Fernandez, the Reverend Richard Hart, the Reverend Donald Jordan, the Reverend Newell Knudson, the Reverend Glenda Thomas, the Reverend Mike M. Morizono, and the Reverend Don Cunningham, conference council director.

Conference church historian Newell P. Knudson, delineating the reasons why Leontine was elected and assigned to the California-Nevada Conference, said:

> Several important factors intersected to make it happen. One was her own sparkling personality and obvious qualifications for leadership. One was the openness of the California-Nevada Conference to receiving the first African-American woman to be elected bishop. The third was the skillful and persistent organization of United Methodist clergywomen, who felt that the time was right to break up the all-male Council of Bishops. There was one other factor, which Kelly puts into words, saying, "if God wanted me to be a bishop, nothing would stop me."[2]

Leontine did not hestitate to demonstrate her spiritual and administrative leadership. She recognized that though she would be bishop for life, her age, by church law, would be a prohibiting factor—allowing only four years of active episcopal service and requiring retirement in 1988. So she concentrated on familiarizing herself with the pastors and congregations under her supervision. She became acquainted with the social, political, and economic issues affecting her constituents and publicly addressed those issues within the annual conference arena and throughout the communities of California and Nevada.

Upon arrival at the conference headquarters, then located in downtown San Francisco at Glide Memorial United Methodist Church, which was pastored by the noted Reverend Cecil Williams, Leontine told reporters at a press conference that although she is the boss she believes in sharing power. "I will not model a leadership role that will not be caring and understanding."[3]

Newell Knudson also noted that one of the first major administrative steps Leontine took in her role as bishop was ensuring that the conference had a strong Evangelism Section of the Conference Board of Discipleship and a strong, highly respected conference lay leader. She persuaded the Reverend John Dodson, pastor at Los Altos, to be chair of the Conference Board of Discipleship and Kimball Salmon, a strong layperson, to serve as conference lay leader. She also facilitated the shift of the conference's fiscal management responsibilities in preparation for the retirement of the Reverend Harry Shaner, conference treasurer and business manager (1975–1988). Raul Alegria, the first Hispanic to serve as conference treasurer, was hired within a time frame that facilitated a smooth and uninterrupted transition.[4]

Leontine used her voice and personality to influence the Council of Bishops as they debated the moral issues of the day and the church's role and responsibilities. Being in the midst of over one hundred active and retired bishops at the bi-annual Council of Bishops meetings, the majority of them being white males over fifty-five years of age, did not appear to intimidate her. Diminutive in statue, five-foot-two, but with a strong prophetic voice, she never failed to get their attention, whether they agreed with her or not! As an active bishop, she served on the executive committee of the Council of Bishops, was president of the six-member Western Jurisdiction College of Bishops, and was assigned to the General Board of Church and Society. In 1986, Leontine addressed the delegates and participants at the fifteenth Assembly of the World Methodist Council, July 22-29, in Nairobi, Kenya. This was another memorable moment in Methodist history. An African American woman bishop speaking to Methodists from around the globe. A world renowned episcopal leader from South Africa, Bishop Desmond Tutu, commented on Bishop Kelly's inspirational remarks made during the Sunday, July 27 worship service: "I would like to give you one very good theological reason why women ought to be ordained, least of all made bishops. It is Bishop Kelly. She was superb. . . . She really made men understand why women say that when God created man she was experimenting!"[5]

At the 1988 General Conference, Leontine had the unique opportunity to preside over the conference session in which the General Board of Higher Education and Ministry formally presented the proposal for The United Methodist Church to establish The Africa University in Mutare, Zimbabwe. This historic legislation, unanimously passed by the delegates, authorized the board to establish the first United Methodist-affiliated, fully accredited university on the continent of Africa. Many felt the presence of the Holy Spirit in that St. Louis convention hall as the mammoth project was approved. For Leontine, it was an emotionally moving moment. There she sat before one thousand delegates and over five thousand observers, an African American woman embodying her own connectedness to the African continent as a descendent of the slaves brought to the Caribbean and the United States. There she sat, a representative of the thousands of African Americans whose parents and relatives had benefitted from the Methodists' commitment and belief in education, their establishment of colleges and universities around the world—particularly the historically black colleges founded in the United States following the Civil War that continued to enable African American students to have access to a quality education. She could sense the presence of the ancestors and "the cloud of witnesses" whose faith, endurance, and trust in God were embodied in those persons who envisioned the university and its contribution to the peoples of Africa.

Leontine's four years of active episcopacy passed quickly. Though there were petitions to the annual and General Conference to have the retirement age requirement for bishops revised with the hope that Bishop Kelly could continue, she officially retired August 31, 1988, at the age of sixty-eight. Leontine had fallen in love with the San Francisco Bay area often saying, "I literally lost my heart to San Francisco." A year after her election, Pam transferred from Spelman College to the University of California, Berkeley, followed in her sister Angella's footsteps and became a member of Delta Sigma Theta Sorority, Inc., graduated, and established her home in the Bay Area. Leontine, having reconnected with cousins from her father's side who resided in San Mateo, purchased a home near her cousins and joined Jones Memorial United Methodist Church in San Francisco.

In the years following her active episcopacy, Leontine continued her work as a preacher, teacher, and social activist. At the request of Neely McCarter, president of Pacific School of Religion in Berkeley, California, formerly her seminary dean when a student at Union Theological Seminary, Leontine agreed to serve as visiting professor of evangelism and witness for two years. Later she served as adjunct professor at Pacific School of Religion and at Hartford Seminary in Hartford, Connecticut. As a social activist, she became president of the AIDS National Interfaith Network (ANIN) and president of the Interreligious Heath Care ACCESS Campaign.

Two special trips led to spiritually rewarding experiences for Leontine, and she marveled at how God had blessed her life in ways she could never have imagined. One trip was a preaching-teaching tour in Japan. Invited by missionary Judy May Newton to be the guest speaker at the annual Missionary Conference held at Kwansei Gakuin's Sengari campus, Leontine arrived in Tokyo on March 13, 1993, and stayed two weeks in the guest house of the Methodist Kwansei Gakuin University in Nishinoyama, a city near Osaka where Leontine lectured. She also preached and lectured at Asagaya Church and at Shibuya Church, participated in the graduation service at Aoyama Gakuin Women's Junior College, spoke in the chapel at Kobe College, and talked to a gathering of the Kansai Women's Theological Group, to Kobe Eiko Church, and to several other groups. Her interpreter, the Reverend Mayumi Tabuchi wrote:

> I was especially happy when Leontine was giving speeches and I was translating at large churches in Japan. If it weren't for her, I would never have experienced such an opportunity to speak in such a place. I felt overjoyed as I stood there facing the huge congregation. Her sermons all had very strong messages, were full of spirituality, and they were brief, compared to sermons in most Japanese churches. They touched the hearts of the people that heard her. As I was translating, her words became my words because I felt that I had taken part in the preparation of the sermon I was translating. I thought that it was God's work, channeled through us.[6]

Her visit to Africa University in Mutare, Zimbabwe, in December 1994 was just as powerful and emotionally fulfilling as her trip to Japan. Due to illness, Leontine was prohibited from attending the official opening and inaugural ceremonies held in April 1994. Invited by the chancellor, Bishop Emilio de Carvalho, and the vice chancellor, the Reverend John Z. Kurewa, to participate in the ceremonies, she had planned to present the university with the official gavel used at the 1988 General Conference when the legislation to establish the university was unanimously approved. As an executive with the General Board of Higher Education and Ministry whose job description includes staff support in the development of the university, I presented the gavel on her behalf. Later, university officials invited Leontine to participate in Africa University's first graduation ceremony, which was held in December 1994.

Mama and I traveled to Zimbabwe and witnessed the graduation of forty students from different countries on the continent of Africa. Tears flowed as she walked on the campus and kissed the ground. She recalled the initial discussions about the feasibility of building a university in Africa and the faith stance that the people of God had taken by supporting the project. The university was in its first stages of construction, and students and faculty were still using the temporary campus facilities when Leontine arrived. Though the administration, student union, and agriculture and natural science buildings had been completed, dormitories were under construction with many additional buildings still in the planning stages. The faculty, staff, and student body was relatively small, but like their Methodist brothers and sisters throughout the world, they had caught the vision of the African bishops and were making the dream a reality.

By December 1999, Africa University had 220 alumni and 871 students enrolled in the five faculties: Faculty of Theology, Faculty of Agriculture and Natural Resources, Faculty of Education, Faculty of Management and Administration, and Faculty of Humanities and Social Sciences. There were sixty-two faculty members, forty permanent lecturers, three visiting lecturers, and nineteen part-time lecturers. Under the leadership of one of the denomination's dedicated volunteer laypersons, Richard Reeves, who chaired the building and grounds committees from 1988 to 1998, the school grounds developed and expanded into a beautiful campus. It included several teaching blocks: The de Carvalho and Kulah Building; the Ireson-Kurewa Center for Agriculture, Natural Resources and Humanities; and the Agriculture Engineering Building; the Student Union building; Kwang Lim Chapel and Library. Nine residential halls and five staff houses were also completed.

By the time Leontine celebrated her eightieth birthday, March 5, 2000, her contributions had been recognized by many religious and civic organizations and by institutions of higher education. In 1993, Garrett-Evangelical Theological Seminary included her portrait in one of four new stained-glass windows located at the rear of the Chapel of the Unnamed Faithful. The windows, dedicated February 11, illustrated women from the Bible, church leaders who reflect the seminary's commitment to ecumenism and inclusiveness, and women historically related to the seminary.

She received more than ten honorary doctorate degrees—the majority of which are from United Methodist colleges and universities. Included in her numerous awards are the Martin Luther King "Drum Major for Justice" and Grass Roots Leadership Awards from the Southern Christian Leadership Conference and *Ebony* magazine's Black Achievement Award in the area of religion. She is featured in Brian Lanker's *I Dream A World: Portraits of Black Women Who Have Changed America* (1989); in *USA Today*'s "And Still We Rise," interviews with fifty black role models; and in *Ladies Home Journal* magazine's "One Hundred Most Important Women in America." At her eightieth birthday party, an endowed scholarship in her name was established at Africa University and in October 2000, she was inducted into the National Women's Hall of Fame in Seneca Falls, New York, joining 157 prominent women who have been inducted since the founding of the Hall of Fame in 1969.

Persons talking with Leontine will inevitably hear her talk about the importance of relationships. Her walls and scrapbooks are replete with photographs of family members, friends, and colleagues. Like most grandmothers she enjoys bragging about her five grandchildren: Angelyn, Tiffany, Faith, John, and Leon. She celebrates the accomplishments of her children and their spouses: Angella; Gloster, Jr., and Yvonne; John David and Staci; and Pamela, and she makes no apologies for sharing their activities with those willing to listen. She also enjoys proclaiming with pride that they are all involved in the Church either professionally or as active members.

Persons who hear her preach seem to remember most her enthusiasm for the gospel of Jesus Christ and her ability to interpret the Word in such a way that it becomes personal to the listener. In those moments when the Spirit no longer allows her to physically remain at the lectern, she begins to walk the aisle, drawing the audience into her closing words from the hymn "How Firm a Foundation," repeating the powerful fourth verse, which is based on a New Testament promise found in 2 Corinthians 12:9, and the fifth stanza, based on Hebrews 13:5. As one listens they know that each stanza has its own special meaning for her journey through life.

When through fiery trials thy pathways shall lie,
my grace, all sufficient, shall be thy supply;
the flame shall not hurt thee; I only design
thy dross to consume, and thy gold to refine.

The soul that on Jesus still leans for repose,
I will not, I will not desert to its foes;
that soul, though all hell should endeavor to
    shake,
I'll never, no, never, no, never forsake.

Notes

1. The Baptism

1. Grant S. Shockley, "The Methodist Episcopal Church: Promise and Peril, 1784–1939," in *Heritage and Hope: The African American Presence in United Methodism,* ed. Grant S. Shockley (Nashville: Abingdon Press, 1991), 57.

2. Ibid., 73.

3. Ibid., 94-95.

4. Ibid., 86-88.

5. Ibid., 67.

6. Harriet H. Beason, Church Historian, *Mount Zion Methodist Episcopal Historical Journal,* 1916–1920.

7. D. E. Skelton, *History of the Lexington Conference* (1950), 79.

8. William Cowper, "God Moves in a Mysterious Way," no. 215, *The Book of Hymns,* official hymnal of The United Methodist Church, General Conference, 1980, Indianapolis, Ind.

2. A Firm Foundation

1. Peter M. Bergman and Mort N. Bergman, *The Chronological History of the Negro in America* (New York: Harper & Row, 1969), 231, 273-75.

2. Ibid., 303, 304.

3. David DeWitt Turpeau, Sr., *Up from the Canebrakes: An Autobiography* (unpublished, 1940), 24-30.

4. Ibid.

5. Ibid., 25-26.

6. Grant Shockley, "The Methodist Episcopal Church: Promise and Peril, 1784–1939," in *Heritage and Hope: The African American Presence in United Methodism,* ed. Grant S. Shockley (Nashville: Abingdon Press, 1991), 81.

7. Shirley B. Porter, *Methodist Memoirs and Village Vignettes* (Mount Kisco United Methodist Church, 1987), 35; James P. Brawley, *Two Centuries of Methodist Concern: Bondage, Freedom, and Education of Black People* (New York: Vantage Press, 1974), 155.

8. John Hope Franklin and Alfred A. Moss, Jr., *From Slavery to Freedom: A History of African Americans*, 7th ed. (New York: McGraw-Hill, 1994), 312.

9. Turpeau, *Up from the Canebrakes*, 36.

10. Ibid., 37.

11. Shirley Porter, Mount Kisco Church History, Album 1.

12. Frederick A. Norwood, *The Story of American Methodism: A History of the United Methodists and Their Relations* (Nashville: Abingdon Press, 1974), 348-49.

13. Ibid., 349, 353.

14. Ibid., 354; See also Donald K. Gorrell, "The Social Creed and Methodism Through Eighty Years," *Methodist History 26:4* (July 1988), 213-28.

15. Washington Annual Conference Methodist Episcopal Church, Minutes, Fifty-Second Session (1915), 94; emphasis added.

16. Harry Carman, Harold Syrett, and Bernard Wishy, *A History of the American People*, vol. 2 (New York: Knopf, 1961).

17. Franklin and Moss, *From Slavery to Freedom*.

18. Kathleen M. Lesko, *Black Georgetown Remembered: A History of Its Black Community from the Founding of the "Town of George" in 1751 to the Present Day* (Washington, D.C.: Georgetown University Press, 1991), 43, 44.

19. Gloster B. Current, Sr., "I Remember 'Papa,' " unpublished biography (Bryant Family Reunion, June 1989).

20. West Texas Conference of the Methodist Episcopal Church, Minutes (1891–93).

21. Lexington Conference Journal of the Methodist Episcopal Church (1912–1923).

22. D. E. Shelton, *History of the Lexington Conference* (1950), 59.

23. Wendell P. Dabney, *Cincinnati's Colored Citizens* (Cincinnati: Dabney Publishing, 1926), 372.

3. Calvary

1. C. Eric Lincoln and Lawrence H. Mamiya, *The Black Church in the African American Experience* (Durham: Duke University Press, 1990), 7.

2. Wendell P. Dabney, *Cincinnati's Colored Citizens: Historical, Sociological, and Biographical* (Cincinnati: Dabney Publishing, 1926), 372.

3. D. Rossman Turpeau, "The Turpeaus: A Family Odyssey," *The Cincinnati Post*, Saturday, February 27, 1988, sec. B, p. 1.

4. Charles L. Blockson, *The Underground Railroad* (New York: Prentice Hall, 1987). "[T]he Underground Railroad, that secret avenue to freedom taken by an increasingly large number of daring runaways from the beginning of the nineteenth century through . . . the decades between the Fugitive Slave Act and the Civil War. . . . Fugitives were hidden in livery stables, attics, and storerooms, under feather beds, in secret passages. . . . The Wesleyan Methodists . . . probably have as legitimate a claim to consistent Railroad activity as the Quakers" (pp. 1-3).

5. Pauline A. Gaskins Mitchell, *The History of Mt. Zion United Methodist Church and Mt. Zion Cemetery*, 175th Anniversary Booklet (1991).

6. Harry Carman, Harold Syrett, and Bernard Wishy, *A History of the American People*, vol. 2, Since 1865, 2d ed., revised (New York: Knopf, 1961), 528.

7. Grant S. Shockley, "The Methodist Episcopal Church: Promise and Peril, 1784–1939," in *Heritage and Hope: The African American Presence in United Methodism*, ed. Grant S. Shockley (Nashville: Abingdon Press, 1991), 88.

8. Ibid., 95-96.

9. Ibid., 90; Shockley, "A Division That Unites: Pride and Perseverance, 1940-1968," in *Heritage and Hope*, 162.

10. Shockley, "The Methodist Episcopal Church," 83, 90, 97.

11. James P. Brawley, *Two Centuries of Methodist Concern: Bondage, Freedom and Education of Black People* (New York: Vantage Press, 1974), 187-88.

12. John Hope Franklin and Alfred A Moss, Jr., *From Slavery to Freedom: A History of African Americans*, 7th Edition (New York: McGraw-Hill, 1994), 383-84.

13. Alan Axelrod and Charles Phillips, *What Every American Should Know About American History: 200 Events That Shaped the Nation* (Holbrook, Mass.: Bob Adams Publishers, 1992), 277.

14. Ibid., 277-79.

15. Franklin and Moss, *From Slavery to Freedom*, 388-89.

16. Philander Smith College (Walden Seminary) was founded by the Freedmen's Aid Society in 1877 and was closely related to the Little Rock Annual Conference of the Methodist Episcopal Church. See James Brawley, *Two Centuries of Methodist Concern*, 433.

4. Unification

1. Frederick A. Norwood, *The Story of American Methodism: A History of the United Methodists and Their Relations* (Nashville: Abingdon Press, 1974), 406-7.

2. Karen Y. Collier, "A Union That Divides: Development of a Church Within a Church," in *Heritage and Hope: The African American*

Presence in United Methodism, ed. Grant S. Shockley (Nashville: Abingdon Press, 1991), 112-13.

3. Lewis V. Baldwin, "Early African American Methodism: Founders and Foundations," in *Heritage and Hope,* 24.

4. James S. Thomas, Methodism's Racial Dilemma: *The Story of the Central Jurisdiction* (Nashville: Abingdon Press, 1992); Grant S. Shockley, "A Division That Unites: Pride and Perseverance, 1940–1968," in *Heritage and Hope,* 120.

5. Norwood, *The Story of American Methodism,* 370-73.

6. Ibid., 407.

7. Collier, "A Union That Divides," 113-14.

8. The National Council of Negro Women was founded in 1935 in New York City; Mary McLeod Bethune was its first president. See *Chronological History of the Negro in America.*

9. Thomas, *Methodism's Racial Dilemma,* 43.

10. James P. Brawley, "Methodist Church from 1939," *Central Christian Advocate* (October 15, 1967): 4.

11. Major J. Jones, "The Central Jurisdiction: Passive Resistance," in *Heritage and Hope,* 196. Collier, "A Union That Divides," 114-15.

12. Ibid.

13. Ibid., 88.

14. Gloster B. Current, Jr., "I Remember 'Papa,'" unpublished biography (Bryant Family Reunion, June 1989), 6.

15. Gloster B. Current, Sr., unpublished autobiography (1979), 35-37. This autobiography is untitled and incomplete. It was intended to be an insider's history of the NAACP from 1941 to 1979.

16. Ibid., 37.

17. John Hope Franklin and Alfred A. Moss, *From Slavery To Freedom: A History of African Americans,* 7th ed. (New York: McGraw-Hill, 1994), 435, 436.

18. Thomas, *Methodism's Racial Dilemma,* 54-55.

19. Journal and Yearbook of the Lexington Conference of the Methodist Episcopal Church, Calvary Methodist Church (Cincinnati, Ohio: April, 1940).

20. Current, Sr., "West Virginia Youth Conference," in unpublished autobiography, 44-45.

21. Grant S. Shockley, "The United Methodist Church: New Church—Old Issues, 1968–Present," in *Heritage and Hope,* 211.

22. Current, Sr., autobiography, 47.

5. New Paths

1. Alvin Burton and Mamie Garvin, *Negro United Methodists in Michigan* (Bryn Mawr, Pa.: Dorrance & Company, 1985), 94-97.

2. Ibid., 95. (This was originally pp. 33-35.)

3. Ibid., 38.

4. Grant S. Shockley, "A Division That Unites: Pride and Perseverance, 1940–1968," in *Heritage and Hope: The African American Presence in United Methodism*, ed. Grant S. Shockley (Nashville: Abingdon Press, 1991), 132-33.

5. Gloster B. Current, Sr., "A Great Membership Campaign and Then the Convention," in unpublished autobiography, 76.

6. *Detroit Tribune*, Saturday, 22 August 1942.

7. Current, Sr., "Return to Detroit," in unpublished autobiography, 50-65.

8. Harry Carman, Harold C. Syrett, and Bernard Wishy, *History of the American People* (New York: Knopf, 1961), 690.

9. Alan Alexrod and Charles Philllips, *What Every American Should Know About American History: 200 Events That Shaped the Nation* (Holbrook, Ma.: Bob Adams, 1992), 289.

10. William B. McClain, *Come Sunday: The Liturgy of Zion* (Nashville: Abingdon Press, 1990), 37.

11. Shockley, "A Division That Unites," 118.

12. James S. Thomas, *Methodism's Racial Dilemma: The Story of the Central Jurisdiction* (Nashville: Abingdon Press, 1992), 80-81.

6. Standing on God's Promises

1. Gloster B. Current, "The Impact of NAACP Conventions on Race Relations," *The Crisis Magazine* 91(7) (August/September 1984).

2. John Hope Franklin and Alfred A. Moss, Jr., *From Slavery to Freedom: A History of African Americans*, 7th ed. (New York: McGraw-Hill, 1994), 492-95.

3. James S. Thomas, *Methodism's Racial Dilemma: The Story of the Central Jurisdiction* (Nashville: Abingdon Press, 1992), 108, quoting Journal of the Sixth Session of the Central Jurisdictional Conference of the Methodist Church (1960), 72.

4. Thomas, *Methodism's Radical Dilemma*, 107-9.

5. Alice G. Knotts, "Thema Stevens, Crusader for Racial Justice," in *Spirituality and Social Responsibility: Vocational Vision of Women in the United Methodist Tradition*, ed. Rosemary Skinner Keller (Nashville: Abingdon Press, 1993), 231.

6. Grant S. Shockley, "A Division That Unites: Pride and Perseverance, 1940–1968," in *Heritage and Hope: The African American Presence in United Methodism*, ed. Grant S. Shockley (Nashville: Abingdon Press, 1991), 134-35.

7. Thomas, *Methodism's Racial Dilemma,* 118-19, quoting "Bridges to Racial Equality," report to the Central Jurisdiction Conference (June 16-21, 1964), Central Jurisdiction Study Committee, 1, 21.

8. Major J. Jones, "The Central Jurisdiction: Passive Resistance," in *Heritage and Hope,* 204.

9. Ibid.

10. Ibid., 205.

11. Thomas, *Methodism Racial Dilemma,* 122, 123.

12. Ibid., 124.

7. Galilee

1. William Ragsdale Cannon, *A Magnificent Obsession: The Autobiography of William Ragsdale Cannon* (Nashville: Abingdon Press, 1999), 242.

2. Leontine T. C. Kelly, conversation with author, December, 1999.

8. Barriers Broken

1. *Daily Christian Advocate,* 3, no.1-A (18 April 1972), proceedings of the General Conference of The United Methodist Church.

2. Grant S. Shockley, "The United Methodist Church: New Church—Old Issues, 1968–Present," in *Heritage and Hope: The African American Presence in United Methodism,* ed. Grant S. Shockley (Nashville: Abingdon Press, 1991), 221.

9. Make Plain the Vision

1. Habakkuk 2:2, RSV.

2. John Hope Franklin and Alfred A. Moss, Jr., *From Slavery to Freedom: A History of African Americans,* 7th ed. (New York: McGraw-Hill, 1994), 524.

3. Proclamation by The United Nations General Assembly, Mexico City, Mexico (1972).

4. *Daily Christian Advocate,* advance ed. (Portland, Ore.: 27 April 1976), J-50, the General Conference of The United Methodist Church.

5. Leontine T. C. Kelly, conversation with author, January 2000.

6. Barbarba B. Troxell, "Honoring One Another with Our Stories: Authority and Mutual Ministry Among United Methodist Clergywomen in the Last Decade of the Twentieth Century," in *Spirituality and Social Responsibility: Vocational Vision of Women in the United Methodist Tradition,* ed. Rosemary Skinner Keller (Nashville: Abingdon Press, 1993), 289.

7. Lynn Norment, *Ebony* (November 1981), 99-104.

8. Liz Lopez Spence, "Calling the Vision," *Make Plain the Vision: A Book of Sermons in Celebration of the Ministry of Women in the United Methodist Church,* ed. Judith L. Weidman (Nashville: Board of Higher Education and Ministry, The United Methodist Church, 1984), 62.

9. Leontine T. C. Kelly, letters to the Reverend Helen Neinast from the Committee for the Episcopal Election of the Reverend Leontine T. C. Kelly (June 25, 1984).

10. Amazing Grace

1. Dewitt Dykes, Jr., "Leontine Kelly (1920–)" in *Notable Black American Women,* ed. Jessie Carney Smith (Detroit: Gale Research Inc., 1992), 623.

2. Newell P. Knudson, *Adventure in Faith: The History of the California-Nevada Conference of the United Methodist Church, 1948–1998* (Visalia, Calif.: Commission on Archives and History, California-Nevada Annual Conference of The United Methodist Church, 1999).

3. Marilyn Marshall, "First Black Woman Bishop," *Ebony* (November 1984), 170.

4. Knudson, *Adventure in Faith,* 211.

5. Dykes, *Notable Black American Women,* 625.

6. Mayumi Tabuchi, "Bishop Leontine Kelly in Japan," (in Japanese) Fukuin to Sekai (August 1993); trans. Hiroko Tabuchi, ed. Judith May Newton (July 1993).

Bibliography

Axelrod, Alan, and Charles Phillips. *What Every American Should Know About American History: 200 Events That Shaped the Nation.* Holbrook, Mass.: Bob Adams Publishers, 1992.

Beason, Harriet H. *Mount Zion Methodist Episcopal Historical Journal* (Washington, D.C., 1916-1920).

Bergman, Peter M., and Mort N. Bergman. *The Chronological History of the Negro in America.* New York: The New American Library, 1969.

Blockson, Charles L. *The Underground Railroad.* New York: Prentice Hall, 1987.

Brawley, James P. *Two Centuries of Methodist Concern: Bondage, Freedom, and Education of Black People.* New York: Vantage Press, 1974.

Burton, Alvin, and Mamie Garvin. *Negro United Methodists in Michigan.* Bryn Mawr, Pa.: Dorrance, 1985.

Cannon, William Ragsdale. *A Magnificent Obsession: The Autobiography of William Ragsdale Cannon.* Nashville: Abingdon Press, 1999.

Carman, Harry, Harold Syrett, and Bernard Wishey. *A History of the American People.* 2 vols. New York: Knopf, 1961.

Current, Gloster B., Sr. "I Remember Papa" (unpublished paper, Bryant Family Reunion, 1989).

———. "The Impact of NAACP Conventions on Race Relations." *The Crisis Magazine* (August/September 1984): 51-58.

———. unpublished autobiography (New York, 1979).

Dabney, Wendell P. *Cincinnati's Colored Citizens.* Cincinnati: Dabney Publishing, 1926.

Daily Christian Advocate. Advance ed. The General Conference of the United Methodist Church (1976).

Daily Christian Advocate. Proceedings of the General Conference of the United Methodist Church (1972).

Dennis, Debra. "The Turpeaus: A Family Odyssey." *The Cincinnati Post.* 27 February 1988.

Franklin, John Hope, and Alfred A. Moss, Jr. *From Slavery to Freedom: A History of African Americans.* 7th ed. New York: McGraw-Hill, 1994.

Gorrell, Donald K. "The Social Creed and Methodism Through Eighty Years," *Methodist History* 26, no. 4 (July 1988).

Keller, Rosemary Skinner, ed. *Spirituality and Social Responsibility: Vocational Vision of Women in The United Methodist Tradition.* Nashville: Abingdon Press, 1993.

Knudson, Newell P. *Adventure in Faith: The History of the California-Nevada Conference of the United Methodist Church, 1948–1998.* Visalia, Calif.: Commission on Archives and History, California-Nevada Conference of the United Methodist Church, 1999.

Lesko, Kathleen M. *Black Georgetown Remembered: A History of Its Black Community from the Founding of the "Town of George" in 1751 to the Present Day.* Washington, D.C.: Georgetown University Press, 1991.

Lexington Conference Journal of the Methodist Episcopal Church, 1912–1923.

Lexington Conference of the Methodist Episcopal Church. Seventy-first session. Journal and yearbook. April, 1940.

Lincoln, C. Eric, and Lawrence H. Mamiya. *The Black Church in the African American Experience.* Durham, N.C.: Duke University Press, 1990.

Marshall, Marilyn. "First Black Woman Bishop." *Ebony* (November 1984): 164-71.

McClain, William B. *Come Sunday: The Liturgy of Zion.* Nashville: Abingdon Press, 1990.

Mitchell, Pauline A. Gaskins. *The History of Mt. Zion United Methodist Church and Mt. Zion Cemetery.* 175th Anniversary Booklet. Washington, D.C., 1991.

Norment, Lynn. "In the Male Domain of Pastoring Women Find Success In The Pulpit." *Ebony* (November 1981): 99-104.

Norwood, Frederick. *The Story of American Methodism: A History of the United Methodists and Their Relations.* Nashville: Abingdon Press, 1974.

Porter, Shirley B., and Marilyn O. Strother. *Methodist Memoirs and Village Vignettes.* Mount Kisco United Methodist Church, New York, 1987.

Shockley, Grant S., ed. *Heritage and Hope: The African American Presence in United Methodism.* Nashville: Abingdon Press, 1991.

Skelton, D. E. *History of the Lexington Conference.* Indianapolis, 1950.

Smith, Jessie Carney, ed. *Notable Black American Women.* Detroit: Gale Research, Inc., 1992.

Spence, Liz Lopez. "Calling The Vision." In *Make Plain the Vision: A Book of Sermons in Celebration of the Ministry of Women in the United Methodist Church*, edited by Judith L. Weidman. Nashville: Board of Higher Education and Ministry, The United Methodist Church, 1984.

Tabuchi, Mayumi. "Bishop Leontine Kelly in Japan." (in Japanese) Fukuin to Sekai (The Gospel and the Word). August 1993. Translated by Hiroko Tabuchi and edited by Judith May Newton (July 1993).

Thomas, James S. *Methodism's Racial Dilemma: The Story of the Central Jurisdiction*. Nashville: Abingdon Press, 1992.

Turpeau, David DeWitt, Sr. *Up From the Canebrakes: An Autobiography*. Cincinnati, 1940.

The United Nations General Assembly. Proclamation. Mexico City, 1972.

Washington Annual Conference Methodist Episcopal Church. Minutes. 52d sess., 1915.

West Texas Annual Conference of the Methodist Episcopal Church. Minutes. 1894.